THE

AGAINST
CASH

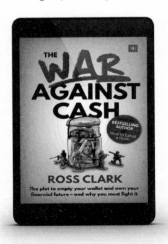

THE WAR AGAINST CASH

The plot to empty your wallet and own your
financial future – and why you must fight it

ROSS CLARK

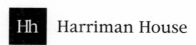

Harriman House

HARRIMAN HOUSE LTD
18 College Street
Petersfield
Hampshire
GU31 4AD
GREAT BRITAIN
Tel: +44 (0)1730 233870

Email: enquiries@harriman-house.com
Website: www.harriman-house.com

First published in Great Britain in 2017.
Copyright © Ross Clark

The right of Ross Clark to be identified as the author has been asserted in accordance with the Copyright, Design and Patents Act 1988.

Paperback ISBN: 978-0-85719-625-5
eBook ISBN: 978-0-85719-626-2

British Library Cataloguing in Publication Data
A CIP catalogue record for this book can be obtained from the British Library.

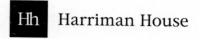 Harriman House

CONTENTS

OTHER BOOKS BY
ROSS CLARK

A Broom Cupboard of One's Own (eBook)

The Great Before (novel)

How to Label a Goat

The Road to Southend Pier

ABOUT THE AUTHOR

ROSS CLARK is a journalist who writes extensively for *The Spectator*, the *Daily Mail*, the *Daily Express* and for many other publications. For many years he wrote the 'Thunderer' column on *The Times*.

Ross is also the bestselling author of *How to Label a Goat: The silly rules and regulations that are strangling Britain*, *The Road to Southend Pier: One man's struggle against the surveillance society*, *A Broom Cupboard of One's Own: The housing crisis and how to solve it*, and *The Great Before*, a satire on the anti-globalisation movement.

CHAPTER

My Little Car Park Problem

I AM STANDING in a car park in Cambridge facing a very simple challenge: can I succeed in paying to park my car in less than the 15 minutes that I want to leave it there? Or rather it would have been simple a couple of weeks ago when the car park still had a functioning ticket machine. Then, all I would have had to have done would have been to slip a few coins in the machine, press a button and out would pop a ticket which I could then put in my windscreen to show to any predatory traffic wardens that I had paid my dues. That is what people have been doing for decades. With no problem at all.

But the ticket machine has been sealed up and a sign taped over it saying:

RINGGO ONLY

RingGo, it turns out, is a mobile phone app which takes cashless payments. I can only park here if I have a mobile phone on me. Happily, I do and, what's more, it is nearly fully charged which is fairly unusual, the charge on a smartphone lasting little more than a day. There is good phone reception here, too, which makes a change from many rural places where I spend time.

There is no Wi-Fi which I can latch onto, however, so the mobile broadband signal had better hold. My web browser still seems poisoned by a Wi-Fi service which I used last week, and which keeps popping up on the screen, even though I am now out of range. But eventually I get rid of it and can look for that RingGo app. I google it and am offered the life and works of Ringo Starr. After scrolling down umpteen references to *Yellow Submarine*, I find the RingGo parking app.

I am away! And only five minutes gone.

But, first, I have to register. It wants to know my mobile number, which I must enter twice on the fiddly little keys on the touch-sensitive screen. I don't know about anyone else, but I find I can hit the right key about two times out of four. Is there anyone with fingers the right size and shape for operating a smartphone keypad? Then I have to enter my name, email address (twice) and then it asks for my Twitter username.

Why?

What the hell has Twitter got to do with it? Then I have to think of a password, which I have to enter twice – while I look anxiously around for traffic wardens. It doesn't like my password, though, because it hasn't got the right number of letters and numerals, so I must think of another – and try to add one more password to my overflowing memory.

Next, I have to enter my car registration number, plus the colour and make of the vehicle, for which I have to scroll down an endless list. Is there really a car called a Burstner, a Jowett or a Gilbern? They sound more like characters from a Tolkienesque underworld.

Ten minutes gone.

And now RingGo wants to know whether I would like to receive a text message whenever my parking time is nearly up (that will be before I have even finished the registration at this rate), and whether I would like to share my email address with 'Trusted Third Party Partners' (do you think I really want to receive junk email?). It wants me to fill in a 'security question' – by entering the characters I can see listed in a box. And then it wants me to enter my credit card number.

My fingers hover over the keys, but then I think the better of it. There is no way that I am going to enter my credit card number into a phone that is not on a secure internet connection. How can I be sure that in one of the other cars in the car park isn't a shady guy on a laptop who is reading everything that I am typing into my phone, and will then swipe hundreds of pounds from my bank account? I can't. I'm not doing it, and so, after 14 minutes of fiddling around I drive off, out to the suburbs where – for now – it still costs nothing to park.

Why have I been put through this tortuous process?

Why can't I pay with cash like I could do until a few weeks ago? According to the City Council, it had its cash machine stolen a few weeks ago. It says it is hoping to install a facility to allow motorists to pay with debit cards. When the parts for the machine arrive from France. But in the meantime, the only option is paying by smartphone – much to the irritation of people who don't have smartphones on them, or who don't own them at all. As for those who have managed successfully to pay, they are complaining that the service keeps adding extra charges, so that half an hour's parking, instead of costing the 90 pence it should have done, has ended up costing £1.50.

What irritates me most, though, is being told that this is all for my convenience.

"So there's no need to fumble with coins in the cold," it says on the RingGo website. "Just download the app and pay for your parking cashlessly instead." They must have a pretty strange set of fingers in RingGo's product development department if they really think it takes less fumbling around to do something on a mobile phone than it does to pick a few coins out of your pocket. Hammersmith and Fulham Council, one of many other authorities which have shifted to cashless parking systems in recent years, declares:

> The frustration of searching for coins in your pocket is set to be a thing of the past. "We are determined to make life easier for residents and visiting shoppers."

Then why not give us a choice of how we want to pay, rather than ripping out the machines?

How often have we been told that the 'cashless society' is coming and it is going to make our lives so much easier?

Apparently, many of us can't wait.

When presented with the statement, "if it were up to me I would go completely cashless," 34 per cent of Europeans agree, according to an Ipsos survey for, er, ING bank.*

As I will explore in this book, an awful lot of the noise about the world going cashless is coming from vested interests: banks, payment companies and other businesses which stand to make more money in a world devoid of cash.

ING was at least game enough to admit that 78 per cent of respondents to its survey said they couldn't imagine the world ever going completely cashless. I am not sure I would count myself in that 78 per cent. I can well imagine cash being withdrawn from circulation. I can foresee governments and big business between them slowly squeezing the usage of cash until it gets to the point

---

* *ING International Survey mobile banking – cashless society*, ING April 2017

at which they can present its ultimate withdrawal as a natural conclusion, a tidying-up exercise which had become inevitable.

We should not allow it to happen.

If we do, we will regret it. What seems at the moment to be a minor irritation – trying to fiddle around with a phone in a cashless car park – would ultimately evolve into a dystopian world in which it dawned on us, too late, that we had ceded huge amounts of control over our lives.

We take cash for granted; it is just there, and we assume it will always be there whether we choose to use it or not. But what if it suddenly wasn't there, if we woke up one morning to discover that the notes and coins in our pockets had suddenly become worthless pieces of paper and metal?

For some, it is not something they have to imagine; it has already happened. I can be relieved that my defining encounter with the cashless society happened in relatively benign circumstances, in a Cambridge car park when I was able to drive off elsewhere and park. It didn't happen, as it did for many poor families, in a village somewhere in Uttar Pradesh, leaving me without any means to buy food, fuel and other basic essentials...

CHAPTER

2

When Cash Stops Flowing

THE BANKS HAD promised to open at 8 am, but by midday their doors were still locked, and queues snaked around the streets of Mumbai. At one of the city's hospitals a new-born baby died while awaiting treatment after the hospital authorities refused to accept the rupee notes which his father, carpenter Jagadish Sharma, proffered as payment.

In the town of Tarapur, 47-year-old farmer Barkit Sheikh, who was desperate for some cash to pay his labourers, collapsed and died after queuing for hours to exchange his suddenly-invalid notes.

The stock market plunged 6 per cent. Shops, cafes and taxis shut up shop, with few able to pay for their services.

It was 8 November 2016, a few hours after Indian Prime Minister Narendra Modi had made the unexpected announcement that 500 and 1,000 rupee notes – representing around 85 per cent of all cash in circulation in the country – would be withdrawn as legal tender with immediate effect. People holding these notes would have until 31 December to present them at a bank, where they could be paid into an account or exchanged for a new issue of notes.

If they brought up to 4,000 rupee worth of notes for exchange, swapping them would be relatively easy, though there would be a few forms to fill in. If they tried to exchange any more than this, they would be subject to inquisition: how had they come by the cash, and why hadn't they paid any tax on it? They would be treated as criminal suspects, in other words, merely because they had chosen to keep some of their savings in cash.

India's demonetisation, as it was called, replicated an exercise in 1946 to rid the country of fortunes made on the black market during the war. The 2016 event was part of Modi's efforts to reduce corruption and tax evasion. In 2010 the World Bank had estimated that the black market accounted for one quarter of the Indian economy, depriving the government of tax revenues and making life difficult for legitimate businesses. Take the notes out of circulation, Modi argued, and fraudsters would find themselves with piles of useless cash which they would be unable to convert into any other form of wealth without alerting the tax authorities.

The government expected that 20 per cent of the withdrawn notes would never be presented to banks,* because their owners were too afraid of the police or the tax authorities to try to exchange them. That, in theory, would mean $40 billion worth of illicit wealth being wiped out.

Many agreed with the project. On the day that the demonetisation was announced, Société Générale put out a note to investors suggesting that it would be good for long-term growth in India. By the end of the year the government was claiming that income tax revenues were up 26 per cent. There were claims that prostitution had declined because potential clients had no means to pay.

Yet as the fallout from the demonetisation started to become clear there was scant sign that criminals had forfeited much wealth. By 31 December 2016, the last date on which the old notes could be exchanged for new ones all but 3 per cent of the old notes had

---

* *India Express*, 5 January 2017

been returned and changed for new ones.* There had been no great wipe-out of criminal wealth. As for the 3 per cent of banknote-wealth which had been lost, it would be rash to assume that all or even most of it had been forfeited by criminals. Much of it must have been lost by ordinary citizens who couldn't access their cash in time to take advantage of the brief opportunity to swap the notes because they were unwell or because they lived too far from a bank branch. As regards to these people, the state effectively just confiscated their wealth.

―――

❝ *The state effectively just confiscated their wealth.* ❞

―――

The whole exercise of demonetisation turned out to be based on a false premise: that criminals hoard vast amounts of cash, and that their activities can be disrupted by removing from them the facility of using cash. Indian tax authorities had already assessed how much illicit wealth was held in the form of cash and come to the conclusion that a maximum of 5 per cent of it was held in the form of 'cash and ornaments'.† Why lump cash with ornaments? The rest was held – like many honest people's wealth – in property, cars, luxury goods and bank accounts.

In return for wiping out a tiny fraction of criminals' wealth, the Modi government caused havoc for the rest of the population, the poor especially.

* *Times of India*, 5 January 2017
† *Hindustan Times*, 16 February 2017

Among those who lost out was Birja, a 32-year-old housemaid in Delhi who had been paid by her employers in expired currency, and who by the end of January had still been unable to cash it in because she had no bank account. Her taxi-driving husband had been hit, too, being unable to find work for the first seven days after the currency had been withdrawn, as people did not have the cash to pay him.

Only about 30 per cent of Indians had access to bank or post office accounts, and so had no alternative way of paying for goods and services. Sixty per cent of migrant workers in Delhi were reported to have left the city as they were not being paid. If prostitution temporarily declined it was only because all industries had suffered from the sudden disappearance of 85 per cent of India's cash. By the middle of January, the World Bank had downgraded its forecast for India's annualised economic growth from 7.6 per cent to 7 per cent.

So much for that banker's note advising people now was the time to invest in India.

The disastrous Indian demonetisation of 2016 gives us a glimpse of what happens when a government decides to withdraw its trusted currency without thinking how, and by whom, cash is used. While the events of November 2016 weren't in themselves orchestrated to turn India cashless overnight – the withdrawn notes were replaced by new notes – the demonetisation was part of a much wider programme by the Indian government eventually to eliminate cash.

Its unashamed "Cashless India" project sets a "vision to transform India into a digitally-empowered society". Companies developing cashless payment systems have been offered tax breaks. Having created havoc for people trying to use cash, on 8 December 2016 the Indian government announced a set of incentives for people paying for goods and services digitally. Central Government Petroleum started to offer a 0.75 per cent discount to motorists buying their fuel by electronic means. The state railway offered 0.5 per cent off tickets which were bought with a card. Buy a ticket online and the railway company would throw in free accident insurance, too. Taken together with the demonetisation it was a pretty unsubtle message to Indians: try to pay with cash and you face nothing but aggro; pay electronically and you will get money off and goodies thrown in. A cynic might just wonder whether a truly modern society would make a greater priority of improving safety on the railways, creating an expectation of finishing a journey in one piece rather than try to entice people to go cashless by offering them free accident insurance.

It isn't just India.

*** Someone, somewhere is coming after the contents of your wallet. ***

While many people remain unaware of it, an increasingly confident propaganda war is being waged against cash worldwide. Someone, somewhere is coming after the contents of your wallet. There is a powerful lobbying operation which wants us to give up the right to pay for stuff with notes and coins and adopt instead an economy where everything is paid for electronically.

Grubby banknotes, they are trying to tell us, belong in a museum. The future belongs to plastic cards – or better still smartphones, wristbands or wearable tags which dock our accounts when we wave them at a receiver. Some even desire to take it to the natural conclusion, and implant wallets in the form of electronic chips beneath our skin.* In 2017, SJ, the Swedish national railway company, started accepting 'tickets' which have been programmed onto microchips implanted into passengers' hands. The system is possible because up to 2,000 Swedes have had the chips implanted as a means of opening security doors and paying for food and drink in their workplace.†

It is all for our convenience, we are told.

❝ *The drive for cashless societies is about one thing above any other: exerting control over us.* ❞

It is about 'empowering' the poor, women especially. It is about fighting criminality. It is the 'modern' way to pay. A 'cashless ecosystem', as the propagandists like to put it, is even good for the environment. Yet these are all dubious claims. The drive for cashless societies is about one thing above any other: exerting control over us, whether it be financial or regulatory control. We are being pushed to go cashless not because it is for our benefit but

---

* *Sydney Morning Herald,* 5 June 2010
† *The Times,* 15 June 2017

because it suits some other, powerful interests who see in a cashless society the chance to make money from us, snoop on us and to steal our savings.

Among those powerful interests are governments.

India is not the only one pushing its people to abandon cash. The Swedish Central Bank withdrew the 1,000 krona note in 2013. Many bank branches there no longer handle cash. Shops and bars now proudly advertise themselves as 'cash-free' zones. The churches have electronic card readers instead of collection plates. Even homeless newspaper vendors have been issued with card readers to take payments via mobile phone. In Denmark, a new law allows shops to accept payments by card only. In 2015 it became illegal in France to settle any bill of 1,000 euros or more in cash; finance minister Michel Sapin declaring that it was necessary to "fight against the use of cash and anonymity in the French economy".* Spain has proposed a similar law. In Louisiana it is now illegal in most cases to buy second-hand goods in cash. In Mexico, cash deposits of over 15,000 pesos are subjected to a tax of 3 per cent. Turkey's Interbank Card Centre, which issues cards on behalf of the country's banks, has launched a single government-approved payment system which it says will become the basis of an entirely cashless economy by 2023.†

In Britain, the government's "digital first" strategy is being used to eliminate notes and coins from transactions where they have always previously been accepted. In London, the buses no longer take cash, only cards from which the fare is docked electronically. The toll booths on the Dartford Crossing have been taken away and motorists are forced to search online for a means to pay.

---

* Reuters, 18 March 2015
† www.troyodeme.com

There is as yet no formal proposal to turn the British economy cashless – Victoria Cleland, the Bank of England's chief cashier, used the occasion of the 50th anniversary of the world's first ATM machine in June 2017 to state that "cash is part of our future plans".* Yet the bank's chief economist Andy Haldane has taken a contradictory view, calling for cash to be eliminated altogether, something he claims would help the Bank fight a future economic crisis.†

Moreover, a Downing Street adviser, Daniel Korski, proposed that the government set a target for turning Britain cashless by 2020. A proposal was due to be unveiled at the Conservative party conference in 2015, but was dropped at the last minute for fear of frightening the public, whom the Chancellor, George Osborne, feared weren't ready for the change. It was put off for another day, and according to Korski there was general excitement in government about the prospect of going cashless in the future.‡ Korski's argument was that abolishing cash would help to fight crime and that such a move "could make Britain the centre for innovation for money in the future" – in other words, the idea had come from the financial technology industry, with little regard to whether the public actually wanted a cashless society.

The case for abolishing cash is backed by Kenneth Rogoff, Professor of Public Policy at Harvard. He has called for governments to phase out cash in order to tackle crime and to give central banks more elbow room in monetary policy – by setting negative interest rates. He demands that the only cash allowed be weighty, low

* BBC, 26 June 2017
† *Financial Times*, 18 September 2015
‡ *The Guardian*, 1 July 2017

denomination coins – such as a dollar piece – of which it would be impossible for anybody to transfer large amounts discreetly but which, he concedes might still allow a child to pop round to the local store to buy an apple.*

The European Commission is also looking into legislation which imposes restrictions on the use cash – based on its claim that "payments in cash are widely used in the financing of terrorism". Under its proposals, either there would be an upper limit on the size of transactions allowed to be conducted in cash or there would be a legal duty, on the part of both payer and payee, to report large cash payments in cash. The Commission has also considered the outright phasing-out of cash – although it recognises that "an important part of the public regards payment by cash as a personal freedom".† It might also consider that terrorists have managed to open and to operate large numbers of bank accounts, often beneath the noses of compliance staff who are supposed to be on the lookout for irregular accounts.‡ So what the EU hopes to achieve through restricting or eliminating cash is not clear.

The United Nations Capital Development Fund has set up a lobbying organisation, the Better Than Cash Alliance, to push towards the elimination of cash. It is backed by 26 governments, including those of India, Pakistan, Kenya, Colombia and Vietnam, as well as charities such as the Bill and Melinda Gates Foundation and businesses which have a rather obvious commercial interest in the death of cash, such as Mastercard and Visa.

---

*   *The Curse of Cash*, Kenneth S. Rogoff

†   *Inception Impact Assessment: proposal for an EU initiative on restrictions on payments in cash*, European Commission, 23 January 2017

‡   *The Times*, 16 November 2016

In its drive to turn the world cashless the Better than Cash Alliance has attempted to lash together as many bandwagons as possible. Among its claims is that a cashless society would aid "women's economic empowerment" – the idea being that wives can't trust their husbands not to steal their hard-earned cash but would struggle to access money stored in their wives' mobile phones. It is an argument which many poor Indian women might find hard to accept, having been messed around and in some cases impoverished by their government's bungled demonetisation. Rural women without access to a bank were some of the biggest victims.

Commercial interests are pushing hard for the abolition of cash. British bank customers are being sent contactless cards – which can be used without a PIN for payments up to £30 – without asking them if they want them or not. In some cases, banks have refused customers an alternative. Fast food chains such as Sweetgreen in the US, and Tossed in Britain, have begun to experiment with restaurants where customers are forced to pay electronically – or go without their salad altogether.

The payments industry is engaged in a huge lobbying operation. There are stalls at political events, sponsored dinners for journalists and policymakers. There are a bewildering numbering of symposiums and conferences where delegates from the payments industry can go to hang out with each other, chomp croissants, sweet-talk civil servants and government ministers, hand each other awards and plot their next assault on the hated enemy: notes and coins. You could fly straight off from the Cashless World conference in Brussels to Cashless Africa at the Lagos Oriental Hotel, then buzz off to the

Cashless Economy gathering in Chennai, India before being back in time for the PayTech conference high up in London's Shard.

❝ Anyone who pays with or accepts cash payments is treated with official suspicion. ❞

Commercial organisations are not shy about what they are trying to achieve. In 2013 management consultants McKinsey produced a paper advising governments on how they could and should be pushing their populations away from cash and towards electronic means of payment. It wasn't enough simply to allow the market for cashless payments to develop, it suggested; there had to be an element of coercion. Governments should embark on a three-phase programme, the first of which was "a long-term plan for discouraging cash use". It went on to label this phase as the "war on cash". As an example of what it meant, it approvingly citied the case of South Korea, where the government has offered businesses a 2 per cent cut on their VAT bill when they take digital payments rather than cash payments. In addition, South Korean merchants who refuse to install card payment terminals are subjected to audits.*

In other words, anyone who pays with or accepts cash payments is treated with official suspicion.

Why the need for coercive tactics if the transition to a cashless society is supposed to be for our benefit?

---

* *McKinsey on Payments*, McKinsey and Company, March 2013

Once you have read the McKinsey report you appreciate exactly what the Indian government was trying to achieve in its demonetisation of 2016. It was straight out of McKinsey's rulebook for waging a "war on cash" – you make life difficult for people trying to pay with notes and coins while at the same time offering financial incentives for people who pay electronically. It might have seemed chaotic, but the more you examine what happened, you more you can determine a scheme.

The fingers of the payments industry can be seen in many places. Visa has started to offer businesses in the US rewards of $10,000 if they agree to update their payment terminals and refuse customers the option of paying with cash. Needless to say, according to Jack Forestell, head of global merchant solutions at the company, it is all in our interests to be forced to pay electronically. "With 70% of the world, or more than five billion people, connected via mobile device by 2020, we have an incredible opportunity to educate merchants and consumers alike on the effectiveness of going cashless," he says.[*] He also suggests that the company is looking at a similar scheme in Britain.[†]

Mastercard has launched a project it calls *The Cashless Journey* which it says will measure the "progress" towards a cashless society. It has divided the world's countries into four groups depending on how advanced they are on what it makes out to be a transition towards enlightenment – based on the percentage of transactions performed with cash. There are countries, like Russia, Italy, Taiwan and Mexico, which it says are on the "inception" of its cashless journey. Next up are countries such as China, Japan, Brazil and

[*] *Fortune,* 13 July 2017
[†] *Daily Mail,* 14 July 2017

Spain, which are in "transition". More enlightened, it claims, are those like USA, Australia, Germany and South Korea which are at the "tipping point" into this golden future. Top of the class are Singapore, Netherlands, France, Sweden and the UK which are "advanced".

But they, too, are too slow for the cashless lobby. Even in the world's most advanced economies, Mastercard is disappointed to observe that 40 per cent of transactions are still done with cash.

Mastercard's *Cashless Journey* makes for some strange bedfellows. In which other list would the US and Germany – respectively the world's and Europe's largest economies – belong in the second rank? In what other context could anyone put Japan – still the world's third largest economy and for decades the powerhouse of the Pacific economy – in the global third division, lagging behind the world's supposedly more advanced nations?

However much Mastercard would like there to be, there simply isn't much of a correlation between the strength and health of an economy and the level of cashless transactions within it. Much of it is just down to national tastes. Germans favour cash more than do the British or the Swedes not because their economy is less advanced but because they are more resistant to any innovation which they feel compromises their personal privacy. They reject credit cards for the same reason that they reject CCTV in the street. They are more inclined, perhaps because of their country's 20th-century history, to see the negative side of surveillance than the positive side.

Why are the French relatively keen on cashless payment methods? Possibly because they have laws which are supposed to limit their workers to a 35–hour week and which has forced the automation of many customer interfaces. Why are the Japanese keen to stick with cash, which still accounts for 80 per cent of transactions in the country?* Perhaps because they are more reluctant than others to apply for credit – it was credit, after all, that was the original driver of plastic money in the 1960s. Moreover, with low levels of crime, the Japanese have never felt so great an incentive to avoid carrying around large quantities of cash. In Japan's case, the low take-up of electronic payment methods is in some ways a symptom of a well-functioning society.

But there is something else.

In the minds of the cashless lobby, Japan is a bovine, backward place – lagging behind not just the likes of Sweden and Singapore but also Kenya, Colombia, the Philippines and all those other developing nations which have signed up for the United Nations' project to turn the world cashless. How can a developed country which transformed manufacturing after the war, which pioneered high-speed trains, transistor radios and so many other electronic goods which came to transform our lives in the second half of the 20th century, be so slow to adopt cashless payment methods?

How can the Japanese be so resistant to enlightened change?

It could be called wisdom.

Japan is no longer the engine of growth it once was. For the past quarter century its economy has struggled, sinking into and out of recession. This reversal has nothing to do with the high level of cash use in the Japanese economy but is the result of the bursting of an unsustainable asset bubble. Japan's once-explosive stock market is still only half the value it was in 1990, its property values have slumped from the days when the grounds of the Emperor's Palace in Tokyo were said to be theoretically worth

---

* Bloomberg, 8 November 2016

more than the entire state of California. In the aftermath of the 1980s boom, Japan became the first major economy in recent times to experience a phenomenon which has since come to visit most developed countries, if briefly: deflation, where the price of goods and assets falls.

Deflation causes misery for borrowers, as the real value of their debts increases year on year. But for savers? It is a boon. As the price of goods and assets falls, the value of money rises. In a deflationary environment a pile of cash is just about the best investment there is. But what if we couldn't keep cash, if there was no cash to keep? Cash held in a bank account is not the same as physical money because it can be manipulated through the device of negative interest rates.

Put £100 in the bank and, rather than see small amounts of interest added month by month, year by year, you would see your money gradually eaten away: maybe £98 next year, £96 the year after. The theory is that this would force us to spend our money rather than squirrelling it away, generating economic activity. Not only that, goes the argument, negative interest rates could help drive up inflation, helping to erode the ever increasing and hard-to-manage debts that are being built up by many governments.

Central banks already have dabbled in negative interest rates. In July 2016 Germany issued a 10-year bond with a negative interest rate for the first time – guaranteeing that the holder will be poorer in a decade's time. The following month, negative rates hit the retail market when a small co-operative bank in the south of the country, Gmund am Tegernsee, levied a rate of minus 0.4 per cent on deposits over 100,000 euros.

But there is a very big block on banks going much further than this: savers have the option of withdrawing their money and keeping it as cash instead. But if cash were discontinued? There would be no bar then to interest rates being set 2, 3, 4 per cent below zero. We would have to grin and bear it because we would have no option to hide our savings under the sofa instead.

The Japanese are well aware of this.

The Bank of Japan has been trying to set negative interest rates for years. In the meantime, the country's savers have been stockpiling cash just in case. In 20 years, the value of notes and coins in circulation has doubled to 101 trillion yen.* When the Bank of Japan finally did set a negative interest rate of 0.1 per cent in January 2016 ordinary depositors were excluded. They had to be, because that would have meant even more cash disappearing from bank accounts, to be squirrelled away in holes and protected from being raided in order to bail out borrowers.

" They have seen the future and it stinks. "

The Japanese are standing up for cash not because they are backward but for the opposite reason: they are more sophisticated than in countries where consumers are being lured to go cashless. In this, the cradle of everything electronic, consumers can see the devious possibilities that would come with a cashless society. They refuse to be manipulated. They have seen the future and it stinks.

* Bloomberg, 8 November 2016

CHAPTER

3

A Matter of Choice

T HERE IS NOTHING wrong with electronic payment methods – when we choose to pay that way. I am not a luddite. I have several debit cards which I use several times a week. I am happy to pay for stuff online because often that is the easiest and quickest way to do so. I regularly transfer money by electronic means. When travelling in London I use an Oyster card, a pre-paid card which allows passengers on the Underground to pay their fare by tapping their card on a yellow circle when they enter and leave a station.

When I bought a house, I didn't turn up at the estate agent's office with several suitcases full of banknotes which I proceeded to count in front of them. That would have been ridiculous; it would have invited someone to cosh me over the head and run away with my suitcases before I had even reached the estate agent's door. I use electronic methods of payment when they suit me; when they are the easiest way to pay. When they are not, I do not use them. Each of us, every day, make decisions as to how to pay for things, and often the choice will come down in favour of paying electronically.

But why the need to force us to pay electronically, to remove from us the option of paying in cash when that is what we want to do?

Why the need to prevent us from storing part of our wealth in the form of cash, if that is what we want to do? The efforts that are being made to remove cash from society are not being done with our consent, or with proper debate as to the consequences; they are being carried out by stealth.

The drive towards a cashless society is something that we need to be aware of and to resist. Just ask yourself: why is it that the people and organisations most evangelical about the cashless society are those in the payments industry? They tell us that a cash-free society would be for our benefit. But it isn't; it is for theirs'. Forcing us onto electronic payment systems allows them to extract money from us in ways that are not possible when we have cash as an alternative.

❝ Why is it that the people and organisations most evangelical about the cashless society are those in the payments industry? ❞

Electronic payment systems allow fees to be creamed off by the middleman, and in ways which those on either side of the transaction hardly notice. Whip out your credit card or debit card in a foreign restaurant, and a fee will end up going to the financial middlemen.

But how much?

You will only find out when you get home and can be bothered to read your bank statement. These fees are not always huge, but if you are making many, small purchases flat-rate fees can add up to large sums. And you can be sure that those fees would grow and grow – and be applied to domestic transactions as well as foreign ones – if paying with cash no longer became an option.

As well as the fees that payment companies can cream off our transactions, cashless payment systems allow us to be mined for data on our spending habits – hugely lucrative for the companies involved but no benefit for us, unless we really want to be bombarded with targeted advertising based on where we have previously spent money.

And for the retail industry, there is another attraction of a cashless society: deprived of cash, they think we might spend more.

As the Dutch banking group ING puts it in a delightfully frank admission:

> Behavioural science suggests that when people do not handle money, they do not feel the 'pain' [of paying for something].*

In other words, commerce wants us to go cashless because it hopes we might be duped into buying things we hadn't intended to buy and spending money that we hadn't intended to spend had we actually had to extract a fiver from our wallet and see it disappear into a till.

Cashless payment systems are all part of the subtle art of getting us to spend more than we really want to. It is like the soothing music played in some stores, or like the chocolates placed by the till so that we might fall for last-minute temptation, or the 'three for the price of two' offers which lead us to buy more than we need.

Cashless payments are designed to work on our psychology. Pay by card or pay by phone and we can be hoodwinked into thinking we haven't handed over anything at. We still have our card, we still have our phone; we can't see that we have sacrificed anything at all.

You won't often hear this point made so honestly by the cashless lobby. Instead, we are showered with spurious reasons why it is in our interests to exchange our wallets for electronic methods

---

* *ING International Survey, mobile banking – cashless society*, ING April 2017

of payment. "There are several reasons to dislike cash," declares Mastercard in the introduction to its *Cashless Journey*. It then goes on to make the startling claim that the existence of cash is placing a burden on national economies of around 1.5 per cent.

It sources this claim to a study published by the Institute for Business in the Global Context at Tufts University, Massachusetts, in 2013. This claims that "[t]he Persistence of a cash economy creates social inequity and has the effect of a regressive tax" – a conclusion it seems to have reached by calculating that poor households in the US pay $4 a month to access cash from cash machines and spend a whopping 28 minutes a month travelling to and from an ATM machine.*

But would they have spent the time productively if they hadn't made the journey? And anyway, what about the ten minutes I wasted in a single afternoon trying to pay by mobile phone for a parking space in Cambridge? Or the 40 minutes I spent the same week on the phone to my bank to unblock my debit card after the bank's anti-fraud department had decided that my attempt to pay my telephone bill might be fraudulent?

The time we waste in trying to cope with awkward and malfunctioning cashless payment systems doesn't seem to have entered into the equation. The idea that 28 minutes spent walking or driving to an ATM is lost time with a value belongs in the world of a corporate bean-counter, not to real people in real life. Many of those journeys to an ATM will have been combined with shopping trips which would have had to have been made whether people needed cash or not. I can't remember a single occasion when I

* *The Cost of Cash in the United States*, Bhaskar Chakravorti and Benjamin D. Mazzotta

travelled to an ATM, withdrew some cash and then returned home without spending any of it or without there being some other purpose to the trip.

As for the fees for accessing our cash from ATMs – fees which few people pay in Britain, so long as they use the chains of ATMs operated by the main banks – it is nothing compared with the costs imposed on people who use mobile phone payment systems in many parts of the world. In Kenya, the poor are paying up to 40 per cent commission on purchases they make via their country's mobile money system M-Pesa – of which more later.

Mastercard goes on to suggest "that heavy usage of cash may be an indicator of other economic problems". That is not an unreasonable point – in Greece, for example, people hold a lot of cash because they are worried that their government will default on its debts, the country will drop out of the euro and the savings in their bank accounts will be devalued.

But how would it help them to remove the option of holding money in cash?

It wouldn't. It would merely ensure that they would end up poorer should their country depart the euro. One might equally say that a government's desire to go cashless can be a symptom of contempt for democracy. Just look at the list of countries which seem keenest to go cashless: Turkey, Ecuador, the Philippines. More on this later, too.

Of all the spurious reasons why societies should go cashless, the one that really took the biscuit for me was a press release from payments company FreedomPay, alleging that cash gives you the flu. "In today's environment of pandemics and epidemics, hospitals are taking a sweeping look at all aspects of reducing chance exposure to bacteria, viruses and other contagions," it reads. Where are they looking? Cash. Money is dirty – in fact, researchers from Applied and Environmental Microbiology report that human influenza viruses can survive on paper currency for as long as 17 days.*

Wow!

Better ditch the cash then and switch to one of those hygienic contactless cards instead, and sponge it down every day with soapy solution. Trouble is that when I've paid for my subway ride I will still have to travel on the same carriage as other sneezing people, cling to the same strap handles as they do. Once I have bought my coffee with my squeaky-clean card I will still have to sit at the same table that was coughed over by someone else a few minutes earlier, sit close to the same air-conditioning duct which sucked in the breath of a tuberculosis victim a few hours before. I will have to tread the same streets scurried over by other people and tread their detritus onto my own carpet when I get home. But, hey, let's heap all the blame for spreading germs on… cash.

If you really want to get away from human germs a better option might be to buy a gun, move to a cabin in backwoods Virginia, and blast at anyone who comes within half a mile. Or maybe just wash your hands before you eat and drink.

While all kinds of spurious reasons are given for abolishing cash, the case for keeping it is really rather simple.

It comes down to the question: do we want governments and a handful of private companies to have complete control over every financial transaction we make – to make money from us every time we buy or sell something, to keep a track of every purchase

---

* Press release, www.freedompay.com, 5 May 2009

we make, and to profit from the sale of the data they collect on our spending habits?

Do we want to give central banks the power to manipulate the economy more than they do already by setting negative interest rates?

Do we want to put ourselves at the mercy of electronic payment systems which can and do fail?

Or do we want to retain the financial resilience, privacy and independence which physical money offers us?

When you start to hack away at the arguments of the cashless lobby you begin to realise what we would lose if we blithely allowed governments and the payments industry between them to wean us off, and then to abolish, cash.

It is not that there is anything magical about cash. It is not something that most of us would want to hold in large quantities. Unless you are a numismatist or a notaphilist – respectively, collectors of coins and banknotes – the physical money we carry around in our pockets, wallets and handbags, is not especially beautiful; it is just an everyday convenience.

At times it has been an astonishingly poor store of value. When I was growing up in the 1970s I liked to count the tuppences in my piggy bank, thinking I was slowly but steadily growing richer. As a nine-year-old I didn't understand how inflation – then 27 per cent – was chipping away at the spending power of those tuppences. In times of high inflation cash was something best held only for short periods.

When the first coins were stamped in the ancient Kingdom of Lydia – now Turkey – in the 7th century BC, they were precious in themselves: they were made from electra, a natural mixture of gold and silver. Already by Roman times, emperors had learned the art of debasing the coinage. They steadily reduced the silver content of denarius from four grams of silver to 0.1 grams.

The Roman public seemed to accept this, and the practice continued throughout medieval Europe. By 1661 the Bank of Stockholm had earned the trust to do what the Chinese had done a thousand years earlier, and introduced paper money. For the next 250 years, banknotes were still linked to the value of gold and silver. But by the 1930s, currency was being decoupled from the value of precious metals for good (although during the commodities' boom of the early 2000s, the materials used to manufacture the English tuppence briefly climbed above the face value of the coin).

From that point on, coins and banknotes have been nothing more than tokens of trust. It is a tribute to the strength and stability of the modern-day nation state and its banking system that virtually all of us are prepared to take currency on trust.

It is remarkable, given the various economic crises of modern times, that money has not suffered more collapses of confidence on the scale of the wealth-destroying Weimar inflation of 1920s Germany. There are hoarders of gold, but many fewer than there were in the high inflation days of the 1960s and 1970s. Come the 1980s and 1990s it was gold rather than cash whose value started melting away in the hand. In 1964, when the James Bond film *Goldfinger* was made, it seemed natural to have a villain who had a Midas-like love of the stuff. Had he not been sucked out of his private jet to oblivion, however, Goldfinger would have ended up on his uppers as the value of gold plunged.

Children need not worry about the contents of their piggy banks any more. Since the economic crash of 2008/09 the value of currency in Western societies has been astonishingly constant – too constant for many governments, who wish they could have a bit of inflation so as to help ease the real value of their debts.

But it isn't the value of physical currency that now causes savers anxiety; more the security of the electronic manifestation of money. In the crisis of 2008/09, many savers were only hours from losing fortunes as banks' balance sheets crumbled and they had to be bailed out. We still use banks, of course, because their services are useful. We are now just more wary of them.

But would we want to be forced to use them, to have them provide the sole means by which we could store our money and take part in the economy?

" The abolition of cash is a solution without a problem. "

The abolition of cash is a solution without a problem. While of course novel forms of doing business will continue to emerge, there is no reason why cash should not remain part of the financial mix – a cheap and easy-to-understand option for paying for things. However much the cashless lobby tries to persuade us otherwise we should cling dearly to our notes and coins, and protest loudly whenever anyone tries to stop us using them. We will regret it if we do not.

CHAPTER

The Cashless Nightmare

T HE DARTFORD CROSSING, on the Thames to the east
of London, is part of the city's orbital motorway. It is also
the only practical way to drive from Kent to Essex. To find an
alternative crossing it is necessary to make a 10–mile detour
through the capital's congested roads. Small wonder, then, that
the crossing – which consists of twin two-lane tunnels to take
northbound traffic and a four-lane bridge to take southbound
traffic – often becomes congested at peak times.

For many years the crossing operated as toll bridges had long
done: motorists drove up to a booth, paid the toll in coins and
waited for the barrier to lift. But in November 2014, the barriers
were removed, allowing motorists to drive straight through. The
toll, however, remained, and motorists are now expected to pay it
online – the system being enforced by cameras which can read the
registration numbers of passing cars. It is still just about possible
to pay the toll by cash, but in order to do so motorists must leave
the road and look for a shop which accepts 'Payzone' payments.
Theoretically, it is also possible to pay by post, but only if you have
paid in advance. If the toll is not paid by midnight on the day after
you have made your crossing you will be sent a £70 fine.

The government claims that as a result of the toll booths being
removed journey times northbound have been reduced by six
minutes and southbound by seven minutes. But that doesn't mean
that the motorists have themselves saved this amount of time

from their schedules. It doesn't include the time that motorists spend paying the toll online, which might require them to find an internet connection while on the move.

By virtue of its position, a significant number of vehicles using the Dartford Crossing are either travelling to or returning from abroad, complicating the process of paying. The inflexible payment arrangements, combined with the short period allowed for payments before a fine is triggered, have resulted in a goldmine for the company which runs the crossing. In less than two years following the removal of the toll barriers 3.5 million fines were issued. Not all the money has, however, been collected – 250,000 fines issued to UK motorists remained unpaid at the end of the first two years of operation.* Many fines issued to foreign motorists have also gone unpaid – although how many we don't know because the government refuses to disclose on the grounds that it might encourage non-payment. In other words, we can take it that huge numbers of drivers of foreign-registered vehicles are not paying, and are getting away with it because it is much harder to pursue them.

Are so many people being fined because they are intentionally trying to use the crossing without paying? Or are they being caught out because they don't know how to pay, they haven't seen or understood the signs? Or they forgot to pay by the deadline? The cashless payment system was promoted as being for motorists' convenience, but in reality it is just a convenient way for the operators to raise money in fines.

The Dartford Crossing is a prime example of the government's "digital by default" strategy – designed to move as many government

* BBC, 9 September 2016

services as possible online. The stated aim is to design "digital services that are so straightforward and convenient that all those who can use them will choose to do so while those who can't are not excluded". Yet, in the event, zeal has taken over. It is straight out of the McKinsey handbook on how to create a cashless society – phase one, the "war on cash".

How easy it would have been to have left two or three toll booths at the Dartford Crossing where cash was accepted – while motorists happy to pay online were able to drive straight through. If it cost a bit more to administer the cash payments, then these costs could easily have been recouped by making the toll slightly higher for people who paid by cash.

What has happened with the Dartford Crossing is so typical of what is happening widely as efforts to force us into a cashless society proceed. The UK government crows that it came top of a United Nations survey for e-government – ahead of Australia and South Korea. The British, apparently, interact with government departments via email and other electronic means more than any other people on earth. Yet the government has never stopped to ask whether e-government is what the population really wants. Cashless payments have been forced upon the public by a generation of policymakers for whom use of computers and mobile phones is second nature, and who spend most of their time in urban areas with good broadband. They have little appreciation of life for those who find it hard to use electronic devices or who live in areas with poor connections.

Cashless payment systems have been introduced despite evidence that they seriously disadvantage the poor and the elderly.

In May 2017, the Office of National Statistics reported that 9 per cent of the British population had never used the internet, either because they found it difficult, they lived in locations which had poor connections or they simply chose not to use it. Ownership of smartphones among 16–24 year olds stood at 90 per cent in 2015. It fell slightly to 87 per cent among 25–34 year olds and 80 per cent among 35–54 year olds. Among 55–64 year olds, however, it slumped to 50 per cent, and among the over-65s it was just 18 per cent.* Yet ignoring this latter figure, Ofcom declared in its 2015 communications report that "[t]he UK is now a smartphone society", as if non-smartphone-users don't exist. Needless to say, the over-65s are the ones most likely to require parking close to shops, doctors' surgeries and so on.

We are with smartphones where we were with motor cars in about the year 1960. At that time, planners worked on the assumption that virtually every household would have a car by some time in the 1980s, and that therefore there was no need to make provision for pedestrians or cyclists, that half the country's railways could be taken up and bus services run down. Yet car ownership in Britain has never advanced beyond 75 per cent of households and belatedly we have realised that car-dependency has created all manner of environmental and social problems – a sensible transport policy makes provision for many alternative forms of getting about. So it will be with smartphones and cashless payments. It may currently seem that they are the future and that all public services should therefore be provided in that way, but in decades to come it will be very clear why we need a plurality of ways to pay for things, cash included.

* *Communications Market Report*, Ofcom 2015

Avril Watson bucked the trend of her age group in that she did own a smartphone when she parked in a Westminster street to go to the theatre. After making a call to an automated line she typed in the registration details, the location code on the sign where she was parked and her credit card details. She did this twice, after being cut off mid-call the first time. An automated voice thanked her very much for using the service – but it didn't stop her receiving a £60 fine. Without a paper ticket, it was hard for her to prove she had paid. It was only after three months of calls to Westminster City Council, and citing proof from her mobile phone company that she had made the call, that the erroneous fine was eventually dropped.*

Who knows why her fine, and many other fines, were issued wrongly. Maybe it was a malfunction in the software configuration to receive the payments; maybe it was the motorist's fault – it is very easy, especially on the touch-sensitive screen of a smartphone, to get one digit of your registration number or their location wrong. But either way, cashless, pay-by-phone systems could not be better designed to entrap the unsuspecting. In 2014/15 Westminster City Council raked in £18 million in parking fines.† Across the country councils between them took £667 million in fines.

Unperturbed by complaints over cashless tolls and parking, a cashless regime will soon be hitting rail passengers, too. The term 'Contactless Transit Framework' means little to the British public, but it is an initiative to do to all public transport what has already been done to the Dartford Crossing: travel will have to be paid for via electronic means, with paying by cash no longer an option. Five

* *Daily Mail*, 3 June 2015
† *Westminster Council Parking Annual Report*, 2014/15

major bus operating companies in Britain have already undertaken to move to cashless payment systems by 2022, with rail travel to follow by 2025.*

The government has warmly embraced the initiative. Rail Minister Claire Perry said in 2016:

> It is a passion of mine to get rid of the tangerine tickets, which look like something out of the 1970s, and move to something that far better suits what customers are using today: mobile technology.

Why her personal distaste for the colour tangerine (tickets of which colour were in fact introduced in the mid-1980s) should justify the abolition of physical railway tickets isn't clear – I fear that if she is ever made food minister she will attempt to ban imports of citrus fruit. But the idea of eliminating cashless payments on public transport wasn't really dreamed up by her, nor by any other government minister. It was not part of any election manifesto. It was not inspired by public demand, nor via public consultation. The Contactless Transit Framework was the brainchild of the UK Cards Association, a trade body which represents the interests of the payment cards industry.

Many passengers might be happy to use their contactless cards, wristbands or any other wearable device to pay to travel on public transport, in which case that is fine for them: let them pay in that way. There are some advantages to this: London's Oyster card system is popular because it obviates the need to queue for a ticket, for example. But the drive to eliminate cash payments altogether ignores the interests of those passengers who do not have bank

---

* *The UK Cards' Association Contactless Transit Project*, press release, May 2016

cards, mobile phones and may not even have bank accounts. While middle-class passengers and policymakers might find it hard to imagine that such people exist, 10 per cent of passengers on Transport for London services have no bank accounts. Needless to say, they tend to be the poorer and older users.*

But it isn't just the poor.

Any of us might find ourselves suddenly without a bank card. It might be cancelled by the bank with no warning and for no obvious reason, requiring us to make long phone calls to get it unblocked. Under the UK Cards Associations' proposals, all rail passengers in future will have to tap in and tap out with their contactless cards – with the card effectively becoming our ticket. Yet at any point on our journey it could become an invalid ticket. Every ten minutes, the computer system would update a 'Deny List' of cards which it had decided were ineligible for travel – the information gleaned from algorithms. The computer might decide, for example, that your card has been stolen because you are making an unusual journey, or made a string of unusual purchases. And if this happens while we are en route, while we are making a journey that we think we have paid for using a contactless card but the card, unknowingly to us, has been added to the deny list? Like the Dartford Crossing's new electronic tolls, Britain's proposed ticketless rail system would be a dream for the ticket inspectors who might then pounce upon us and fine us.

The UK Cards Association's proposals for ticketless travel also includes the facility for paying with our mobile phones or other hand-held devices. Here, too, it is not difficult to guess

* *Contactless Prepaid and Bankcards in Transit Fare Collections Systems*, Candace Elizabeth Blackwood, John Hopkins University 2010

what will happen. Passengers will be fined because their mobile phone batteries have died and they can't show they have bought a ticket, or because they are travelling in a location with no internet connection and have forgotten to download the ticket while they had the chance. Under laws governing rail travel in Britain it is a criminal offence to be unable to show a valid ticket when asked – even if you have actually paid and you can prove it at a later date. And boy, do rail companies take advantage of this.

As in Britain, the public in Sweden is forever being told that cashless payments are all for their convenience – when experience says the opposite. In 2016, Camilla Kristensson did as she had always done: she drove to the local bank to deposit 20,000 krona raised from a village fair in the south of the country. Only this time the bank refused to take the money. Like many banks in Sweden, and with little in the way of announcement, it had suddenly decided to stop handling cash. Her only option was to drive for 40 minutes to a bank in the nearest city. Sweden boasts of being the most cash-free society on earth, with 59 per cent of transactions now done electronically, more than any other country.* An increasing number of shops, bars and hotels now refuse to take cash in payment.

Yet this is not a change driven by public demand; it is being carried out by stealth by the banks themselves. They banded together to introduce a mobile phone-based cashless payment system, called Swish and, once that had been established, started to withdraw cash services from their branches. It is being carried out against the wishes of bodies such as the National Small Business Association, which observes that 53,000 Swedes now have to travel more than 18 miles to access cash from a bank or an ATM.

* *Measuring Progress Towards a Cashless Society*, Mastercard

Why drive cash from society?

Mats Torstendahl, an executive vice-president at Skandinaviska Enskilda Banken, one of Sweden's largest banks, puts it succinctly – and very honestly – telling a reporter from *The New Yorker* in 2016:

> We don't add any value by handing over cash over the counter.*

But when you start to force people to use electronic banking? All sorts of fees then become possible. No one should be fooled if some electronic payment methods do not involve direct charges on the buyer. Whether they would remain free if cash were to be abolished for good is another question. In any case, there are already hidden costs. The Swish phone app is currently free for individuals transferring money between themselves. Businesses, though, pay 1.5–2 Swedish krona per transaction. These costs are, inevitably, passed on to the consumer.

❝ Banks extract over $1 trillion in revenues a year from over $400 trillion of annual payments. ❞

The profits which the payments industry expects to make from shifting society towards cashless forms of payments has already been factored into their business plans. According to a report on the financial technology (fintech) industry put out by the US Department of Commerce's International Trade Administration

* *The New Yorker*, 10 October 2016

in 2016, investors ploughed $19 billion into the sector in 2014. Needless to say, they would only have done that in expectation of a handsome return. The report goes on:

> Banks extract over $1 trillion in revenues a year from over $400 trillion of annual payments, according to the Boston Consulting Group. As consumers in both rich and poor countries increasingly pay with credit cards or online and on their mobile phones, that figure could reach over $2 trillion by 2023.*

No prizes for guessing where that extra £1 trillion is going to come from: you and me. If people willingly want to pay more in order to pay in ways which they personally find more convenient, fair enough. If people find it exciting to use the latest gizmo to pay for their croissant, that is their business. If they want to show off to their friends that they can pay for a taxi ride by waving their designer wristband at the taxi I wouldn't want to deny them their fun. But if we don't stick up for cash now we will find ourselves paying dearly in the longer run.

There is so much money riding on the fintech sector that one senses it is not going to be left to the whim of our personal choice whether to use cashless methods of payment or not – the industry can be relied upon to do all it can to make them compulsory.

We would be more reluctant to go cashless if we realised how much it is already costing us. In Britain, consumers don't usually pay charges for transactions they make on debit cards (credit cards, of course, are another story with their alluring interest-free period followed by extraordinary rates of interest). What few realise is

---

* *Top Markets Report, Financial Technology*, Department of Commerce International Trade Administration, 2016

how much the retailer is paying to accept electronic payments. Handling cash also has a cost, of course: notes and coins have to be counted, transported to the bank and deposited. The cashless lobby likes to talk-up these costs, but they are far less than the fees incurred in handling card payments. According to the British Retail Consortium, retail outlets in Britain in 2015 paid an average of 1.39 pence for handling transactions in cash (equivalent to 0.15 per cent of the value of the transaction). Each debit card transaction cost 5.79 pence (0.22 per cent) and each credit card transaction 28.41 pence (0.79 per cent).* These extra costs, of course, are eventually passed on to the consumer in the form of higher prices.

" The campaign for society to go cashless plays into the hands of big business. "

What the above figures don't tell you is how costs fall disproportionately on small businesses. If you are a high-street store handling thousands of transactions a week, the hire of the terminals required to accept card payments is small relative to the value of the transactions you are handling. But if you are a small shop handling a few transactions a day it is a very large proportion of your costs. The campaign for society to go cashless plays into the hands of big business, which of course loves life to be made difficult for its smaller competitors.

---

* *Payments Survey 2015*, British Retail Consortium

Fees for using contactless cards have already been sneaked onto Australians' shopping bills. Those shopping in Aldi have found themselves charged a fee equivalent to half a per cent of their bill. In Westfield car parks contactless cards incur a fee of 2.5 per cent, and paying for a taxi can incur a charge equivalent to 10 per cent of the fare.[*]

How can companies get away with these extra charges?

Because people using contactless cards get used to tapping them without bothering to check how much they are being charged. The increased speed of the transaction isn't so much for our benefit; by hustling us through the checkout more quickly commercial organisations create an environment in which we don't bother to check the bill.

If you are visiting Sweden and don't have a Swedish bank account the world's most cashless society is already a pretty expensive place to go shopping – and somewhat opaquely so. Armed with a Visa debit card I went there myself in June 2016 when the foreign exchange tables were indicating there were just under 12 krona (SEK) to the pound. As soon as I arrived I withdrew 2,000 SEK from an ATM in Stockholm's Gamla Stan, the old town. Before I committed to the purchase the machine made it clear what exchange rate I would get. My bank statement records that I was charged £170.86 for the transaction, plus a £1.50 'foreign cash fee' levied by Visa. That gave me an effective exchange rate of 11.6 SEK to the pound.

That evening I ate with my wife in a Stockholm restaurant which did still accept cash. Two days later we returned and ordered exactly the same meal, but this time I paid with my Visa card. Notionally,

[*] *Daily Mail,* 22 June 2016

I had received a better exchange rate of 11.9 SEK to the pound, but there was a sting. I was also charged a 2.75 per cent fee plus a £1.50 'non-sterling purchase fee'. This brought my effective exchange rate down to 11.1 SEK to the pound. Worse, neither of these charges was indicated to me at the point of sale – I only discovered these charges on my bank statement when I got home.

The following day we visited the Vasa museum – dedicated to the salvaged remains of Gustav II Adolf's warship which sank in the city's harbour on its maiden voyage in 1628. I paid for the tickets – 130 SEK each – with my Visa card, and faced the same charges. This time, my effective exchange rate was a more miserable-still 10.8 SEK to the pound. The smaller the transaction, the bigger the impact of the £1.50 non-sterling purchase fee. Had I bought a coffee with my card the fees would have doubled the cost of the drink. For the moment, these charges are only levied on foreign cards, but if cash were to be abolished altogether you can guess these are the sort of charges that domestic consumers would be paying, too.

Just along the quayside from the Vasa Museum stands a temple to 1970s glamour: a museum dedicated to the history of the pop group Abba, where you can gawp at shoulder pads and insert yourself into an Abba video. Here, paying with cash is not an option. The museum is backed by Bjorn Ulvaeus, who was one of the members of the band (the one without the beard) but who has reinvented himself as a campaigner for the elimination of cash, a cause to which he says he dedicated himself after his son's flat was burgled in 2010. Given that the burglars took no money, only a TV, computer and designer clothes, it isn't obvious why the abolition of cash would help prevent such a crime, but never mind. Ulvaeus gives his own, convoluted explanation on the museum's website:

We can be reasonably sure that the thieves went straight to their local peddler. We can be absolutely sure that the ensuing exchange of goods never would have taken place in a cashless society.

How come?

Say the thieves had sold the television to a criminal associate using the Swish app on their mobile phones. There would be a record of that transaction, but how on earth would the police link it to the theft? It would hardly be flagged up on the Swish database with the words "sale of Mr Ulvaeus's son's TV" – it would merely be one of many millions of transactions made that day. If the police managed to find a suspect for the theft – say from fingerprints left behind in the flat – they might then look through his Swish records to find that he had received a payment a day or two after the theft. But then he might have received dozens of payments – and none of them would be labelled 'TV' or give any other clue as to what they were for.

Bjorn Ulvaeus's sermon concludes:

> I challenge anyone to come up with reasons to keep cash that outweigh the enormous benefits of getting rid of it. Imagine the worldwide suffering because of crime, from murder to bicycle theft.

Okay, how's this for a reason, Bjorn: I want to keep cash as an option for paying bills so that the banks can't grab us by the short and curlies and add on 'cash fees', 'purchase fees' and all kinds of other levies that they absolutely, certainly will dream up as soon as they feel they can get away with it. I don't want banks to have a monopoly over every small purchase I make. There is nothing in it for me to cede this power to them. I can already buy almost whatever I want with electronic money, should I choose to pay that way. But for me to have to rely on my bank card when the bank's electronic systems could go down – as they frequently do – or to rely on my phone to pay for things when the battery could run down? No thanks.

Cash is what gives us power over the banking industry. It is our alternative, the means by which we can opt out of the services of these monopolistic corporations. Knowing that we can withdraw our money, keep it elsewhere and do business with each other without adding value to the banks' balance sheets is what keeps their charges within reason, concentrates their mind on providing a half-decent service, stops them from helping themselves to as much of our money as they feel like. We would be mad to give in to their crusade to abolish cash and put ourselves at their mercy.

❝ Cash is what gives us power over the banking industry. ❞

When it comes to dreaming up fees to add on the bill, Ulvaeus's museum is a prime example. You can buy your ticket for 195 SEK online or you can pay at the desk for an extra 20 SEK 'service fee'. That is exactly the sort of practice which will become endemic if we allow cash to become extinct. The cashless society is a middleman's dream.

As for the rather goofy premise that ridding the world of cash will also rid it of all crime, from murder to bicycle theft, I wonder whether Bjorn would ever have come up with his campaign if, instead of having his computer stolen, his son had fallen victim to a phishing scam and had money scooped out of his bank account electronically and spirited off through a web of bank accounts which might theoretically be traceable but in practice so rarely seem to get traced.

Bjorn may preach about a golden, cashless future, but for a growing number of the world's criminals the cashless age has already arrived. Not for them stealing the odd bicycle; what's the point when you can cream someone's life savings by planting a bit of malware on their computer? Are the banks going to help you if you find yourself in this position? Don't bet on it. Like many before you, you may find yourself mugged in cyberspace, your bank washing its hand of the crime and the police showing not one jot of interest.

How much you might wish, then, that like your grandparents before you, you had kept at least some of your money rolled up in a jar at the back of the understairs cupboard.

CHAPTER

5

Crime

I AM TRYING to think if I have ever seen a £50 note. Apparently, it is red and until 2014 carried an image of the equally obscure Sir John Houblon (1632–1712), the first governor of the Bank of England. A new note issued in that year bears instead the images of steam-engine-builders James Watt and Matthew Boulton. If the Bank of England has a sense of humour the next £50 note will have a picture of Ronnie Biggs, because that is more in keeping with the reputation of the thing.

What legitimate reason, asks the anti-cash lobby, is there for the vast number of banknotes in circulation? As of 2016 there was £67.8 billion worth of sterling banknotes in circulation, up from £36.9 billion a decade earlier. That works out at over £1,000 for every man, woman and child in Britain.

Where is it all?

It isn't in my wallet. Like most people I rarely have more than £100 on me, and there is another £100 somewhere in my house which I once hid, in case of emergencies, in a very special place – so special that I can't now remember where it was. As for the elusive £50 note, there are £13 billion worth of them kicking around somewhere, and neither I nor anyone else seems to have much idea where they are.

It is a similar story with the US dollar, only more so. In 2015 there were $1.34 trillion worth of dollar bills at large in society – i.e. not held in bank vaults. That works out at $4,200 for every man, woman and child in the US. And yet a survey in 2012 claimed that Americans had an average of only $46 in their wallets.*

How come the discrepancy?

Moreover, where are all the $100 bills which ordinary citizens seem rarely to see and yet which make up 80 per cent of the dollar bills in circulation? Can it be that while you and I go about with our fivers and tenners there is a vast underground, illegal economy feeding on this vast surfeit of cash?

That is what some believe. "There is little question that cash plays a starring role in a broad range of criminal activities," writes Kenneth Rogoff in his book *The Curse of Cash*, "including drug trafficking, racketeering, extortion, corruption of public officials, human trafficking and, of course, money laundering". What more proof could you need of the evils of cash than the discovery of $200 million in cash found at the home of Mexican drug lord 'El Chapo' Guzman, arrested in Mexico in 2014?

Rogoff's assertion is straightforward: cash makes life easy for criminals. It helps them cover up their dodgy dealings and hide transactions from the taxman and the police. If they couldn't pay each other in cash, their lives would be more difficult. Eliminating cash altogether would therefore cut crime.

Or maybe it wouldn't.

In reality there is a lot less cash in illicit circulation than the above figures might suggest. Moreover, vast amounts of crime are committed using a means of exchange other than banknotes.

To take the first of these points, it is erroneous to divide the total number of US dollars in circulation by the population of the US and use that figure as an indication of some vast

* *The Curse of Cash*, Kenneth S. Rogoff

underground stash of cash in the country. The dollar is an international reserve currency, used as a second currency all around the world in the same way that English is used as a second language. At least seven countries, including Ecuador, East Timor, El Salvador and Zimbabwe have adopted it as their official currency. According to the US Federal Reserve, around 65 per cent of all US banknotes are held by individuals and organisations outside the US. Once you take that into account, the amount of cash apparently being held, per capita, by US citizens falls from $4,200 to $1,470.

As for the $100 notes, the proportion the Fed Reserve believes to be held abroad is 75 per cent.* That large quantities of dollars are held abroad is not a function of criminality. There are perfectly legitimate reasons for citizens and businesses around the world to want to hold dollars: it is a far more reliable store of wealth, compared with local currency, in countries which have suffered from inflation and political turmoil. More on this later.

As for the assertion that cash can be equated with crime, this would be more convincing if criminals didn't also have bank accounts, properties, cars, bling and all manner of other ways of storing their ill-gotten wealth. Of course, criminals use cash, but for them, as for the rest of us, it is only part of the story.

Another part of it is the top-end London properties which the police are now coming around to realise are being used as a store of wealth for the world's criminals. In 2015, Donald Toon, head of Britain's National Crime Agency, told the *Financial Times*: "The London property market has been skewed by laundered money.

---

* *Current Issues in Economics and Finance*, Federal Reserve Bank of New York, January 2010

Prices are being artificially driven up by overseas criminals who want to sequester their assets in the UK".*

But these assets weren't bought with banknotes. No one can walk into a London estate agent and buy a property with bags full of cash: the estate agents are under legal obligation to report anyone who tries to do this. These properties were bought via large cash transfers from overseas banks: electronic money.

Maybe the criminals should not have been allowed to open these bank accounts; perhaps someone had not done due diligence and checked the provenance of the money in these accounts, or possibly there are criminals working inside the banking system who facilitated them. Yet the fact is that they did open them. So long as criminals are able to open bank accounts with impunity, eliminating cash from circulation is going to make minimal difference to the amount of crime.

Rogoff's case would be stronger were it not for the astonishing amount of fraud which takes place online, involving electronic money. Where, in the argument that associates cash with crime, fits the shocking statistic that in 2015 British bank customers lost a total of £755 million in fraud involving payment cards, online banking and (the last making up a very small proportion of the total) cheques?† None of those thefts involved criminals carrying around cash in their swag bags; it was siphoned off from customers electronically, into bank accounts which fraudsters had somehow managed to open regardless of the mechanisms which are supposed to be in place to stop them.

---

* *Financial Times*, 6 April 2016
† *Fraud: the Facts 2016, the definitive overview of payments industry fraud*, Financial Fraud Action UK

The argument that cash encourages crime and that creating a cashless society would cut crime is based on the idea that cash is untraceable, whereas electronic money leaves a trail which can be picked up by law enforcement authorities.

The first assertion is not entirely true: there is technology which can keep some kind of trace on banknotes, if not every transaction, by automated reading of serial numbers of banknotes. In 2013, a German company, C I Tech Components, launched a reader which can be incorporated into an ATM and used to record the serial numbers of every banknote dispensed to an individual – information which might be of use if the banknotes later turn up in the clutches of a criminal.* There are also various products on the market which have been used to tag banknotes stolen from security vans – and which will invisibly stain the hands and clothes of the thieves.

As for the second assertion, that is true in theory. But just because electronic money leaves a trail as it pads around the economy doesn't mean that the police, or anyone else, actually has their sniffer dogs on it. True, if you ring the police to report that you have had stolen a large sum of money which you had carefully sewn into your mattress you are unlikely to get a positive response, still less are you likely to see your cash again. But are you any more likely to recover a large sum of money which you have had stolen from your bank account by electronic means?

The supposed traceability of electronic money didn't help Andrew Doyle and Susan Paul who in 2016 were defrauded of £204,390 which they were trying to transfer to their solicitors as a deposit for buying a home in Wiltshire. Their solicitor had said that he would

* www.atmmarketplace.com, 19 August 2013

email the bank account number and sort code. An email arrived in Mr Doyle's inbox giving the details of an account, to which Mr Doyle sent the money. Only later did he discover that somewhere along the line fraudsters had hacked into the emails between him and his solicitor, and given him their own bank account details. By the time he knew about the fraud, his money had been whisked away electronically, not to be seen by him again.*

It is a form of fraud which has been repeated numerous times – and yet still criminals seem able to pull it off, via bank accounts which are theoretically traceable, but in practice no law enforcement body seems able or bothered to do the tracing. How Mr Doyle must wish he had visited his solicitor in person and dumped a suitcase full of banknotes on the floor. He might have put himself at the risk of being mugged but the result could not have been worse than what did actually happen to him.

Edward Smith, too, learned the hard way about the supposed traceability of electronic money. When, in 2016, he received a text message purporting to be from his bank, Santander, and asking that they call him about an alleged attempt to access his bank account, he did as he was asked. Why shouldn't he, given that the message seemed to be included amid a legitimate string of messages from the bank? When he called he was fooled into parting with vital information "to get past security". That done, fraudsters duly emptied his bank account of £23,000 – and Santander refused to refund him a penny on the basis that the fraudsters had not hacked into their computer systems – rather they had used a technique called 'smishing' to fool his phone into thinking the message had come from Santander.†

* *Daily Telegraph*, 23 April 2016
† *Daily Mail*, 21 March 2017

There are cases, too, like that of Alex Luke, who lost £180,000 from her account after she received a call from a man purporting to be a technician working for her internet provider. He said he had rung to alert her that criminals had targeted her bank account. That much was true; what she didn't realise, as she was asked to log onto her computer and perform various operations to test whether anyone had managed to access her account, was that she was talking to the fraudster himself. Having obtained the passwords he required, he then stripped her account via 33 different transactions over the following 24 hours, taking between £6,000 and £8,000 each time. Once again, although the criminals' transactions were theoretically traceable, the money was not traced.*

It is easy to attack victims such as these for their credulity, but the fraudsters are employing ever more devious ways of obtaining the details they need. In Luke's case, she handed control of her computer over to the man claiming to be a technician – something which many people are requested to do, quite legitimately, when sorting out technical problems with their devices. Fraudsters have devised devious ways of convincing people they are talking to their bank. A favourite ruse is to invite their victim to call back on the bank's – genuine – number. However, the fraudster stays on the line, so they don't get through to their bank at all.

But even if you are minded to pour scorn on the victims for being so foolish, is it really acceptable that so many people are falling victim to online fraud?

How would abolishing cash help end this kind of fraud?
It wouldn't.

* *Daily Mail*, 29 March 2017

Far from it, all it would do is to force millions of people who do not feel confident using computers to start using online banking. Hard though it might be for those in the professional classes to comprehend, according to the House of Commons Science and Technological Select Committee, 5.8 million Britons have never used the internet. In a cashless society, these people would be sitting ducks for fraud.

" In a cashless society, people less confident with computers would be sitting ducks for fraud. "

In any case, however careful bank customers are they can't guard against falling victims to attacks on the banks' own computer systems. Hacking directly into bank accounts is happening on an industrial scale, and the banking industry is struggling to keep up.

In November 2016 Tesco Bank announced that 20,000 of its customers' accounts had been raided and small amounts of cash extracted from each one. The customers in this case were refunded by the bank, but their faith in electronic money can hardly have been enhanced.*

Online fraud has long eclipsed physical theft of money. In the year to September 2016, according to the National Audit Office (NAO), there were 623,000 recorded online frauds in Britain. Many thefts, though, go unreported. The NAO estimates there

* Reuters, 7 November 2016

were a total of 1.9 million in the year to September 2016, accounting for 16 per cent of all crime. The most prevalent – accounting for 1.4 million crimes – is 'card not present' fraud – where criminals manage to obtain the number, sort code and security code of a debit or credit card and then use it to buy things or transfer money online.* In order to commit this kind of crime it is only necessary to have possession of a card for a minute or so – long enough to write down the numbers. Alternatively, the information can be obtained via malware installed on a computer.

I offer my own observations to back the NAO's assertion that online fraud is now much bigger than physical burglary and theft. I have been carrying cash around in my wallet all my adult life. Never have I had so much as a £5 note stolen. No one has ever seized my wallet nor taken my cashpoint card. I have never been followed to a cashpoint machine. I was once approached by muggers who asked if I had a mobile phone and would I like to give it to them (they didn't even ask for cash) and I told them to bugger off (they did). My house has never been broken into. My car was broken into once but the thieves found nothing except the handbook, which they dumped on the road.

As for attempted electronic crime, I must receive a minimum of ten emails every day trying to pull off frauds against me. Two or three times a week I receive phone calls from people purporting to be from my internet provider and trying to pull off the same trick as they did against Alex Luke. That gives an idea of the scale of the criminal operation trying night and day to part us from our electronic money. It is a vast, terrifying world where your life savings can be spirited away to a distant country in the blink of an

* *Online Fraud*, National Audit Office, 30 June 2017

eye, and where no authority seems to bother itself much to seek out the electronic fingerprints.

In Britain, according to the NAO, only one in 150 police officers are dedicated to online crime. Only 27 out of 41 Police and Crime Commissioners even referred to online fraud in their police and crime plans – an annual statement laying out their priorities and how they intend to pursue them. As Amyas Morse, Britain's grandly-named Comptroller and Auditor General put it:

> For too long as a low value but high-volume crime, online fraud has been overlooked by government, law enforcement and industry.*

And still the anti-cash lobby tries to convince us that it is the few banknotes in our pockets which are the real risk; get rid of them and we will never live with the threat of crime again. It is an argument utterly without foundation.

It isn't just online banking which has become a target for fraudsters. Whole new possibilities for crime have arisen with contactless cards – the technology with which the banks and payments industry is trying to wean us off cash. The cards, fixed with small wireless receivers, allow payments to be made by merely tapping a card against a terminal containing a small transmitter. They do away with the need to enter a PIN every time we use a card – a measure which, like everything else in the cashless payments industry, is supposed to be for our convenience.

But contactless cards are proving mighty convenient for criminals, too. As with banknotes, anyone in possession of a contactless card can use it to make purchases. The difference is that anyone who finds or steals your wallet can only spend the money contained

---

* National Audit Office press release, 30 June 2017

within it. Find or steal a contactless card, on the other hand, and a criminal can spend the entire contents of your bank account. In Britain, for example, contactless cards can be used for payments of up to £30 with no proof of identity required.

Contactless cards are proving mighty convenient for criminals.

Bank customers are finding themselves falling victim to fraud on their contactless cards even after reporting them lost or stolen. Criminals can still use the cards after they have been cancelled on a bank's computer system because 45 per cent of purchases are made offline – that is to say the payments are not actually processed until several hours after the card has been tapped on a card reader. In such circumstances, there is no way for the shop, at the point of sale, to know that a card has been cancelled. To the thief it is effectively like a wallet stuffed with an exceptionally large wad of cash.*

Criminals don't necessarily even have to take physical possession of your card. A device found in circulation in the South London criminal underworld has been found to be capable of skimming sufficient information from a contactless card which comes within several centimetres of it to produce a cloned card.† In Australia,

---

* Letter from chairman of Treasury Select Committee to Financial Services Authority, 2 February 2017
† *Daily Mail*, 12 June 2016

where the equivalent PayPass cards can be used for purchases of up to $100, police have attributed a sharp rise in car break-ins to criminal gangs out to steal the cards.*

The cards' industry claims to guard against fraud on contactless cards in two ways: by setting a limit on the value of a purchase which can be made with the cards when in contactless mode (currently £30 in the UK) and by programming regular checks. Every so often – the card industry won't reveal how often, for fear the information might be useful for fraudsters – the user will be asked to enter a PIN. However, most contactless cards can also be used online in contactless mode, where there is no spending limit and no requirement for a PIN.

Researchers from *Which* magazine bought a simple card scanner from a mainstream source and managed to use it to skim sufficient information from a card which came into close contact to create a cloned card. They then used the cloned card to buy a £3,000 television online.†

How close does your contactless card need to come in contact with a scanner to be vulnerable in this way? The cards industry says that contactless cards are designed to be read from a maximum of 5 cm but, according to the National Consumers Federation in the US, some can be read from 15 to 20 cm away. Travelling on crowded trains or standing in cafe queues there are going to be many occasions when your card might potentially come within reading distance of a scanner hidden in someone else's bag.

When challenged on fraud, the payments industry likes to quote a figure claiming that only 0.5 per cent of card fraud is done on

* *Daily Mail*, 24 November 2015
† *The Guardian*, 23 July 2015

contactless cards.* It is a familiar trick: reduce something down to what sounds a reassuringly small number. But it is a meaningless statistic, not least because most new cards can operate in contactless mode but can also be used online, or over the phone, or in chip and pin mode. If data is skimmed from your card via a scanner and then used online to buy a television, is that contactless card fraud or just ordinary card fraud? It is both.

How prevalent is card fraud compared with the theft of physical money?

According to the Office of National Statistics 4.6 per cent of adults reported falling victim to fraud involving plastic cards in 2014/15.† By contrast, 0.7 per cent of adults reported falling victim to theft from the person and 1.5 per cent of adults reported falling victim to other theft of personal property.‡ The latter two figures do not just include thefts of cash; they also include thefts of mobile phones, jewellery and all manner of other things.

It is clear from this that significantly greater numbers of people are suffering from fraud connected to plastic cards than are having cash stolen from their wallets, their homes, their cars or anywhere else.

As in Britain, so in the US: it is online and card fraud, not the physical theft of cash, which is the real problem. Only 1.8 per cent of US households a year report any kind of cash theft – whether from the person, the home or a vehicle. The total cash reported stolen from private individuals totals $500 million – a grand total

---

* *Fraud, the Facts*, Financial Fraud Action UK
† *Patterns and Trends in Property Crime*, Office of National Statistics, 2015
‡ *Focus on Property Crime*, Office of National Statistics, March 2016

of $1.60 per American.* Considering the billions of dollars which Americans are accused of hoarding, it is a tiny sum.

The argument that we need to abandon cash in favour of supposedly more secure cashless payment systems to protect us from having our money pilfered does not stand up to examination.

There are several other ways in which using cash might protect you against crime. If you buy a second-hand car with cash, you can complete the deal instantly – you check the paperwork, take the car and the seller takes the money. Try to do the transaction electronically and it requires an element of trust. Transfer money to a seller's bank account before you see the car and you may never get to see the car at all.

The internet is awash with fraudsters who are happy to take an electronic payment for goods or services which they then fail to deliver. In the first nine months of 2015 PayPal was reported to have experienced a fraud rate of 0.28 per cent while its rival Square had a fraud rate of 0.16 per cent. The latter lost $5.7 million from one merchant alone, who had sold travel vouchers which turned out to be bogus.†

Accepting payments by card is equally fraught with the risk of theft. Contactless cards may give the seller the impression that a transaction has been instantly completed, and that it is irreversible. But this is not quite the case. The seller can hand over goods or provide a service in return for what seems like a secure payment – only to find that the money has been clawed back. As the UK Cards Association notes on its website, in its advice to merchants:

---

* *The Cost of Cash in the United States*, Bhaskar Chakravorti and Benjamin D. Mazzotta, 2013

† *Forbes*, 13 November 2015

In the majority of cases, the terminal will provide an authorisation when a transaction is processed. This confirms at that time that the card used has not been reported as lost or stolen and that there are sufficient funds available in the cardholder's account to make the purchase. However, this is not a guarantee that the transaction will ultimately be paid as it may be charged back due to a variety of reasons.

In other words: you might think you've got the money, but don't count on it – we might snatch it back if there is some kind of irregularity. How much you might wish you had been paid with a bunch of fivers instead.

CHAPTER

The Big Guys

I F BRITAIN'S £50 notes are fairly elusive, the same is even more so of the European Central Bank's high-denomination euro notes. Little known to European citizens and to tourists, who are unlikely to have handled anything more than a 50 euro note, the European Central Bank issued – until 2016 – a 500 euro note, in purple, with an imaginary cable-stayed bridge on one side and a glass edifice on the other. The note was withdrawn because of increasing fears that it was being used by criminals. It had even acquired a nickname, the 'Bin Laden'.

The argument against large-denomination banknotes has been laid out in a paper by Peter Sands of Harvard Kennedy School.* An amount of $1 million in $20 bills, he noted, weighs 110 lbs and fills four briefcases. In $100 bills it weighs 22 lbs and fills one briefcase. In 500 euro notes, by contrast, it weighs just 5lbs and can be squashed in an airline cabin bag. Sands then lists some of the seizures of cash in recent years, from 6.1 million euros worth of 500 euro notes seized by US federal agents in 2007 and linked to a cocaine money-laundering scheme, to 200,000 euros worth of 500 euro notes found in the stomach of a "euro mule" in 2004. A traveller in Mexico, he adds, was caught with $151,000 worth of dollar bills thanks to a cash detector dog – a breed of pooch trained to sniff out large quantities of the ink used

* 'Making it Harder for the Bad Guys', Harvard Kennedy School, February 2016

in manufacturing banknotes, now being used by police forces around the world.

By contrast, he asserts, look how difficult it is to carry around large amounts of cash in China, where the highest denomination note in circulation is worth only $16. Although that hasn't stopped some criminals: a general arrested in 2014 for taking bribes in return for promotions was found to have so much cash in his house that it took 12 trucks to remove it.

The argument that equates cash with crime would stand up better if it weren't equally possible to list large numbers of cases where criminals have laundered money through bank accounts, with not a single banknote involved. The $200 million of banknotes found at El Chapo's home is small beer compared with the vast quantities of money which are being laundered through bank accounts. In 2012 HSBC was fined $1.9 billion after a US Senate Investigation concluded that the bank had been a "conduit for drug kingpins and rogue nations". Among its failures were allowing Mexican and Colombian drugs cartels to launder $881 million through accounts, and to allow a Russian gang posing as second-hand car dealers to transfer $290 million.* According to the Organized Crime and Corruption Reports Project, 17 UK-based banks between them unwittingly processed $738 million worth of transactions on behalf of Russian criminal gangs. They didn't need to move banknotes around in bags: they processed the money electronically through anonymous companies which they then dissolved.†

I guess that El Chapo was really just the criminal world's equivalent of your granny: he stuck with cash because it was

---

* Reuters, 11 December 2012
† *The Guardian*, 21 March 2017

what he knew. Meanwhile, younger rivals have had little trouble mastering the banking system to their advantage. They don't even have to fear the dreaded cash detector dog. If only we had dogs intelligent enough to sit at a computer and sniff out suspicious online transactions we might be closer to tackling fraud.

It shouldn't be possible for a criminal gang to open a bank account in Britain. Banks are obliged to undertake due diligence when anyone opens a bank account: to check the identity of the applicant and to satisfy themselves that the quantity of money involved is consistent with their identity. If a 19-year-old student attempted to open a bank account with half a million pounds it ought to raise the alarm. Yet criminals manage to shift money around by hijacking other people's accounts.

International students are a favourite target. Sometimes the criminals do it with the permission of the students, sometimes not. In one case, an Indian student who found himself struggling with living costs in London was offered £500 if he would pass his account number and sort code to a third party. He did so, despite guessing that the account would then be used for illegal transfers. In another case, a mechanical engineering student was surprised, when he checked his account, to find that £10,000 had suddenly been paid into his account, by whom he had no idea. Within a day, £50,000 had been transferred through his account.* He had no idea how the criminals had obtained his bank account details, but it needn't have taxed them greatly. All they would have had to do was briefly to gain possession of one of his bank statements or his bank card – easy to do, for example, if the gang has someone working as a waiter in a busy restaurant, who will arouse little

* BBC *Inside Out*, 12 September 2016

suspicion if he takes away the card in order to enact payment for a meal.

Or the gang might have used a malicious software called Dridex, which the student might have innocently opened in an email attachment, allowing the criminals access to bank account details. That was the method used by Moldovian nationals Pavel Gincota and Ion Turean, jailed in October 2016 for laundering £2.5 million through 220 bank accounts of unwitting accomplices.*

There are other ways, too.

Criminals often succeed in opening bank accounts by applying directly to banks under false identities. They might begin with store loyalty cards, which are easy to obtain, and use them to build up a pattern of spending in order to fool a bank into allowing them to open a current account. They might steal letters delivered to properties in multiple occupation. According to the credit agency Experian, 89 out of every 10,000 current account applications in Britain are fraudulent.†

What, then, does it add to the fight against crime to ban large denomination banknotes?

Little or nothing.

It might be a minor inconvenience for some criminals used to handling cash, but they will soon adjust to using bank accounts as many are already doing. Any who are still using cash will retire their suitcases and violin cases and instead pick up the art of using malicious software to access the accounts of honest citizens and use them to spirit vast sums across borders; just as many of their criminal associates are already doing. Can the

* National Crime Agency press release, 5 October 2016
† *Financial Times*, 1 July 2015

world's anti-fraud squads catch up? Not on current evidence they can't.

To be fair to Peter Sands, he didn't propose the total abolition of cash in his Harvard Kennedy School paper; just large-denomination notes. Moreover, he also recognised that not everyone with a few $100 bills sewn in their mattress is necessarily a criminal. "There probably is some legitimate hoarding of cash," he writes. But how much cash holding is legitimate and how much criminal? He admits that he has no idea. "For high denomination notes there is even less data than on cash in general," he writes. "It is remarkable how little we know about the whereabouts and utilization of a product created and distributed by the state."

In which case why assume that most of it is in the paws of criminals? The discrepancy between how much cash people say they have in their wallets and how much cash is actually in circulation cannot be taken as evidence of mass criminality. Why would anyone who is hoarding cash want to share that information with an opinion pollster? You can't really expect people, when cold-called or stopped in the street and asked how much cash they keep in their wallet, their car or their house to make an honest response: "I've got three grand stashed in a tub of ice cream in the freezer and another five grand in the grandfather clock".

People are shy enough when telling pollsters how they intend to vote – with the result that polls in many recent elections have proved spectacularly wrong. You might as well stand in the high street and ask passers-by for the PIN to their bank card. They are not going to tell you.

If people have taken to hoarding cash in increasing quantities over the past few years it isn't hard to see why: they don't trust banks.

And with very good reason.

CHAPTER

7

Who Would Trust a Bank?

U NTIL 14 SEPTEMBER 2007 a bank run was a thing of history; an event which might have happened in the 19th-century Wild West but not something which happened in an advanced industrialised country like Britain. There were enough things to worry about in economic life – inflation, stock market crashes, a slide in the pound – but the safety of deposits in British banks was not one of them.

Yet by the end of that day customers of Northern Rock – a former mutual building society which had become a bank a decade earlier and grown with great confidence since – had collectively withdrawn £1 billion worth of savings. Queues had reached around the block. At one point in Kingston, Surrey, 250 customers had been queueing. At branches in Sheffield and Golders Green police were called to keep order. In Cheltenham, a retired hotelier and his wife refused to leave the bank until they were allowed to withdraw their entire £1 million savings.* In an effort to convince customers that it wasn't about to slam its doors, Northern Rock kept some of its branches open until half past ten in the evening.

Yet to no avail: the next day, Saturday, saw even bigger crowds and a further £1 billion withdrawn.

It wasn't until the evening of the following Monday, when the Chancellor of the Exchequer, Alistair Darling, announced that the government would underwrite all deposits at Northern Rock, that

* *Daily Telegraph*, 14 September 2007

the panic subsided – although that came at the cost of causing problems for other banks and building societies as Northern Rock suddenly went from being the most risky place to put your savings to the least risky.

What had started the run?

An announcement on the Friday morning that Northern Rock had had to go to the Bank of England for an emergency loan. For years, Northern Rock had grown by committing what for many older bankers was regarded as a cardinal sin: borrowing short and lending long. It advanced mortgages at attractive interest rates for terms of 25 years, but relied on financing those loans by taking out a series of short-term loans. That was fine so long as interest rates remained low and credit markets functioned well. It meant disaster if, as happened on 9 August 2007, global credit markets froze in reaction to worries over the health of US mortgage securities. Too many US house-buyers had been granted too many mortgages at terms that were too favourable – and their loans bundled up and sold on as quality bonds, when in fact the homebuyers behind them were struggling to pay the interest and defaulting.

Throughout the run on Northern Rock, figures of authority had sought to present it as an irrational panic. Alistair Darling tried to reassure the country that the bank was solvent. The Chairman of the House of Commons Treasury Select Committee, John McFall, announced that the "banking system was strong". Angela Knight, chief executive of the British Bankers Association – a trade body – said: "Everyone should calm down and refrain from making simplistic comments in a very complex area which cause unnecessary concern".

It wasn't until a week later that the governor of the Bank of England, Mervyn King, admitted to MPs that Northern Rock customers queueing to get their money out had been acting rationally.* At the time, the government had a scheme for bailing out customers of collapsed banks: it would compensate them for the first £2,000 of their savings to the tune of 100 per cent. The next £33,000 worth of savings would be reimbursed at 90 per cent.

Trouble was, many Northern Rock customers had deposits well in excess of £35,000. Had the bank failed they would have lost tens of thousands, and in some cases hundreds of thousands of pounds. For some months, Northern Rock was widely assumed to have unique problems. But a year later the entire banking system came close to collapse when the full extent of the US mortgage securities scandal was becoming clear and one bank after another was forced to go cap in hand to the Bank of England to seek emergency funding or a full-scale bail-out.

What happened to the money that was withdrawn?

Much of it, no doubt, was paid into accounts with other banks, which were at first widely assumed not to suffer from the same problems as Northern Rock. Some was invested in gold – the price of which rose from $650 an ounce in September 2007 to over $1900 an ounce in 2011. Some went into property – although the housing market fell sharply in 2008. But some, inevitably, went into banknotes. How much, nobody knows. But the Bank of England recorded massive rises in the quantity of banknotes in circulation in the two years following the Northern Rock disaster: from £38.4 billion at the end of February 2007 to £44.9 billion 12

* *The Run on the Rock*, House of Commons Treasury Select Committee, 2008

months later and £48.6 billion 12 months after that. In the three years prior to 2007 the amount of cash in circulation had been fairly steady: between February 2004 and February 2005 it had actually fallen by £600 million.

Here are the Bank of England's figures for cash in circulation at the end of February in each year:*

2004	£36.016 bn
2005	£35.415 bn
2006	£36.913 bn
2007	£38.449 bn
2008	£44.979 bn
2009	£48.608 bn
2010	£50.220 bn
2011	£52.194 bn
2012	£54.921 bn

Anyone who assumes that the large quantities of cash being held by the public must be a symptom of drug crime or tax evasion has to ask themselves: why did the number of banknotes suddenly ratchet up immediately after the Northern Rock disaster? Did the British public suddenly discover an appetite for criminality or were many scared by what they had witnessed and decide to engage in what Peter Sands referred to as "legitimate hoarding"?

No one knows the extent of hoarding of cash, though the Bank of England has had a go at guessing the minds of cash-hoarders. It estimates hoarding of sterling at £3 billion, with an average of £345 "per hoarder".

---

* Banknote statistics, Bank of England website

Does that level of cash-retention really deserve to be called "hoarding", though?

Surely for many households it is just a week's worth of expenditure. Would we describe someone as a hoarder just because they kept a week's worth of food in the freezer? Of course not, so why does someone who keeps a week's worth of spending money deserve to go by that name? When the Bank asked in a survey why people kept cash at home 18 per cent said the prime motivation was pure convenience: they kept it for potential emergencies.*

Keeping notes and coins surely only deserves to be called hoarding when it involves thousands of pounds. No one, short of dismantling a sample of British houses or digging up a sample of gardens to find concealed cash, is ever going to come up with an accurate estimate for how much of this goes on. But the £10 billion uplift in cash in circulation during the banking crisis and its immediate aftermath is as good a guide as we'll get.

In October 2008, the amount of an individual's savings which the government agreed to refund in the event of a banking collapse was increased to £50,000, and was later increased further still to £85,000. Yet still that was little comfort to depositors with sums in excess of this.

The whole banking crisis provided a sharp reminder that bank deposits were far from risk-free. Burying a pile of money in your garden, or hiding it in your house, is also risky, of course. But it doesn't leave you exposed to the global financial forces which brought down Northern Rock and which few people understand – including, it seemed, the board of Northern Rock. Neither, as mentioned in the previous chapter, is there much evidence that

* *Bank of England Quarterly Bulletin*, Quarter 3 2015

individuals are losing significant sums of cash to theft. If you are what the Bank of England calls a "super-hoarder", with more than £100,000 squirrelled away in your home, it is a fair bet that you have invested in a safe – the same device, if on a smaller scale, as banks use to keep their cash from being pilfered. It is the things we use in everyday life and consequently don't hide away – the car, the television, etc. – which are far more vulnerable to theft.

In any case, if people want to run the risk of having cash stolen from them, it is their choice. Why take away the facility of the public to hoard banknotes? Why make us utterly dependent on banks when the banks have come so close to losing their customers their deposits?

It is easy to see from the banks' point of view why they would favour this arrangement – it would give them access to tens of billions of pounds of deposits, currently being held in banknotes, on which they would need to pay little or no interest. But for the rest of us there is no advantage to being forced to deposit our savings in a bank account. On the contrary, to have the option to withdraw our money and keep it as cash – even if we don't actually choose to do this – gives us a power over the banks that we would not have in a cashless society.

It is no coincidence that the countries with the lowest proportion of cashless transactions are Italy (6 per cent) and Greece (2 per cent).* Both countries have suffered sovereign debt crises which has led many to fear that they will crash out of the euro. If they did do this, they would be forced to adopt new national currencies at a much-devalued rate. Wealth held in the form of bank deposits would be eroded in euro terms but wealth held in the form of banknotes would be retained – it would have to, because those

* *Measuring Progress Toward a Cashless Society*, Mastercard

notes would remain legal tender throughout the rest of Europe and, in spite of slight differences in design between notes issued in different eurozone countries, no government nor the European Central Bank could be sure whether any particular note had been held in Greece by a Greek citizen, in Italy by an Italian or by a German in Germany. For Greeks and Italians banknotes offer a security which bank accounts do not. That is a security which the anti-cash lobby wants to take away from them.

❝ For Greeks and Italians banknotes offer a security which bank accounts do not. ❞

Why, of all countries, is it Swedish banks which seem keenest to eradicate the use of cash?

Once it was Sweden which had Europe's dodgiest banks. Banking deregulation in 1985 led to a boom in lending which, by the early 1990s, began to go bad as interest rates rose and borrowers struggled to service their loans. In the spring of 1992 the insurance company which was the majority owner of the Gota Bank announced that it was running out of resources to prop up the bank. Over the following week, in a foretaste of the Northern Rock crisis, its customers withdrew 5 per cent of its deposits. Those who got their money out early were the wise ones: at the time, there was no formal deposit guarantee scheme in Sweden. Depositors were only saved when on 9 September Gota Bank was taken over by the state-owned Nordbanken.

But the crisis didn't end there.

A week later the withdrawal of sterling from the EU's Exchange Rate Mechanism – which pegged a number of European currencies to the Deutschmark – forced Sweden's central bank, the Riksbank to increase interest rates to head off a run on the krona. All Swedish banks were now in trouble, and the government was forced to guarantee all bank deposits and bail out the banks with emergency funding.

Twenty-five years on there is little sign of humility among Swedish banks. On the contrary, they are prime-movers behind a drive to make the country the world's first cashless nation.

It is they who – jointly – launched the mobile phone app known as Swish, which allows instant transfers of money, requiring senders and receiver merely to exchange phone numbers. The app is now used by half the Swedish population.

According to the Riksbank, cash now accounts for just 2 per cent of transactions by value.[*] In contrast to most countries the quantity of banknotes in circulation in Sweden is in decline, falling from 106 billion krona in 2009 to 80 billion in 2015. Swedish banks are forcing the switch to cashless payment by removing ATMs and shutting their cash facilities: 900 of the country's 1600 bank branches now refuse to handle any kind of cash. They like to boast of an incident in 2013 when the world's most hapless bank robber burst into a Stockholm branch of Enskilda Banken and demanded cash, only to be told there was none[†] – like a pub with no beer, this was a bank with no money.

* *The Guardian*, 4 June 2016
† *Wired*, May 2016

The number of bank robberies has plummeted: according to the Swedish National Council for Crime Prevention there were only 23 raids across the entire country in 2014, down by 70 per cent in ten years. What the banks are less keen to point out is that the decline in bank robberies has been accompanied by a sharp rise in online fraud: in 2013, the year that Swish was introduced, internet fraud rose 37 per cent in 12 months.*

The decline in bank robberies is reassuring if you are a bank cashier, but the cashless society that Sweden is becoming is less good news for the customer.

Swish is most popular among young people: a generation who were not born at the time of the 1992 crisis or who were too young to remember it. They will not know what it is like to fear for your savings.

Older Swedes who do remember 1992 tend to take a different view. They are more likely to be drawn to a pressure group called Cash Uprising which has formed to fight what it sees as a forced and hurried change to cashless payment systems.

Whether they keep much of their savings in the form of banknotes or not, for them cash is a potential last resort. It offers them resilience in the event of a repeat of the 1992 crisis. When the very organisations which caused that crisis through reckless lending try to force them to give up cash, they smell a very large rat.

---

* www.scancomark.com, 11 July 2013

CHAPTER

Tax Evasion

I N FEBRUARY 2015, the rather miserable little hedge outside Ed Balls's East London home briefly became the epicentre of British political debate. Balls, then shadow chancellor in the opposition Labour party, had decided to tackle the subject of tax evasion. He said:

> I think the right thing to do if you are having somebody to cut your hedge for a tenner is to make sure that they give you their name and address and receipt so there's a record that you paid them.

The tabloids immediately embarked on the hunt for Mr Balls's hedge-cutter. He remained elusive, but the *Daily Mail* found his window-cleaner, who insisted that Mr Balls had never asked for a receipt for his £12-a-month cleaning service – a bill Balls always paid by cheque.* David Cameron, then prime minister, waded into the debate along with many others, to protest that the customers of small businesses have every right to pay them in whatever form they like. They were not expected to do the work of Her Majesty's Revenue and Customs for it by sniffing out suspected tax-dodgers.

True, there is a chance that the tenner you press into the paw of an odd-job man might not find its way into his books – if he keeps any books. It might get spent in the pub on the way home, without the taxman getting his cut.

* *Daily Mail*, 17 February 2015

But what Balls was doing is what many in the anti-cash lobby have done: to imply that tax-dodging is endemic among small tradesmen, an accusation he would be less inclined to make of large corporations. If Mr Balls paid a tenner for a pair of socks in a high street store would he similarly make sure he kept the receipt, on the suspicion that the shop was evading its taxes?

Of course he wouldn't.

When we pay for things in a chain store we take it for granted that tax will be paid – even though deep down we must know that big businesses don't like paying tax any more than does the small guy, and are far more inventive in finding ways to avoid it. What caused outrage at Ed Balls's remarks is that at the same time he was casting suspicion in small tradesmen, huge corporations were getting away with paying tiny tax bills. Their means might be legal, involving the fertile imaginations of accountants, but the end result is the same: the government doesn't get the tax revenues for which it thought it had made provision.

The battle against tax evasion is one of the chief arguments employed by the anti-cash lobby. Force cash out of existence, goes the argument, and no one will be able to slip that tenner in their back pocket without informing the taxman. All payments will have to go through the books and be recorded in some electronic form, for tax inspectors to pore over should they take a fancy.

There are plenty of fanciful estimates of the money being lost to governments as a result of tax evasion in a giant underground, cash economy.

The US Institute for Business in the Global Context thinks that the US tax authorities are losing between $100 billion and $200 billion in tax revenues a year thanks to people doing business on the sly courtesy of banknotes and brown envelopes.* The range of these estimates tells you all you need to know: they are pretty wild guesses. The upper figure is devised from an estimate by the Internal Revenue Service (IRS) of a $376 billion annual 'tax gap' in the US (the difference between what the IRS takes in revenue and what it thinks it ought to be taking) combined with a guess by the National Tax Advocate that 52 per cent of missing tax can be attributed to under-reporting of income by self-employed taxpayers.

Even assuming that these figures are anywhere close to the truth – which is quite an 'if' – is it really fair to blame all this tax evasion on the existence of cash?

It is possible, of course, to fiddle your taxes using a bank account – such as by hiving payments into a number of different accounts, by taking payments via a PayPal account in a false name, or holding them in another country. Abolishing cash might make it riskier in some ways to under-report income, but then it is hardly risk-free evading tax by taking large quantities in cash. Suspected tax-dodgers can be, and are, easily caught out by the taxman through sending a snoop to undertake a test-purchase: just ask the suspected tax-dodger, nod, nod, wink, wink, if he will knock a bit off the bill if you pay in cash and, if he says yes, you've caught him.

That tradesmen and other small businesses are taking payments in cash is not in itself evidence of tax avoidance, whatever some will say. There are good reasons why your gardener, your cleaner or odd-job man might prefer to be paid in cash, and which have nothing to do with trying to evade tax. It is hard for tradesmen

* *The Cost of Cash in the United States*, Bhaskar Chakravorti and Benjamin D. Mazzotta, 2013

to ask to be paid upfront, as larger businesses can demand. It is usual practice for plumbers, etc. to be paid at the end of a job after the householder has been able to inspect the work. A cheque from a trusted customer might be acceptable – even if it involves an unwanted trip to the bank – but it is certain that sooner or later the tradesman is going to have a few bounced cheques on his hands, involving time and expense trying to extract payment.

Small businesses like cash because it is instant and there is no risk that a payment can fail at a later stage. To accuse them of tax-dodging is a calumny which tends to be spread by people who have never run a business relying on collecting money in arrears.

What the abolition of cash would not achieve is to tackle the more significant end of tax-dodging: the corporate end, with its diverted profits and its obscure offshore structures.

There are equally wild estimates available estimating the amount of money lost to the taxpayer of corporate tax avoidance. You can take your pick: Oxfam reckons that US corporations keep a £1 trillion offshore for tax purposes, resulting in a cost to the US taxpayer of $111 billion.* The European Commission estimates that aggressive tax avoidance costs European governments 70 billion euros annually.† I am not going to take these too seriously, but it is quite clear that there is a vast amount of tax evasion/aggressive avoidance going on and a lot of practices which stand in a grey area in the middle which do not involve cash and which authorities have nevertheless struggled to tackle.

---

* *The Atlantic*, 14 April 2016
† *Financial Times*, 28 January 2016

As with criminal gangs defrauding us online, just because a transaction is electronic and therefore theoretically traceable does not necessarily mean that anyone has succeeded in tracing it.

_____

❝ *Countering tax evasion is yet one more spurious argument employed by the cashless lobby.* ❞

_____

What does distinguish electronic money is that it is far easier to shift abroad than cash. The ability to move money around the world quickly and seamlessly has hugely facilitated tax avoidance. Abolish cash and you might tackle a little bit of petty tax evasion at the lower end of the spectrum, but the serious end will continue to grow. Countering tax evasion is yet one more spurious argument employed by the cashless lobby, when really it has ulterior motives.

CHAPTER

9

Dependency

JUST WHAT WOULD happen in a cashless society if, as in Britain in 2008 or Sweden in 1992, the banks came close to insolvency and all electronic payment systems froze – either as a result of technological failure or cyber-attack?

Nobody quite knows, of course, because the world does not yet have a cashless society. But we have had plenty of small foretastes of what could be to come.

In June 2012 a technician in Hyderabad made an error while inputting data for an upgrade to computer systems for the Royal Bank of Scotland (RBS). The following day some of the ten million account holders with RBS-owned NatWest and Ulster Bank began to report problems making card payments or withdrawing cash from ATMs.

Customers were left unable to do their shopping, or to buy petrol to get home. Some discovered that payments for direct debit had been taken from their accounts twice, forcing them into overdraft. Some faced fines or interest charges for being unable to meet payment deadlines. Travellers were stranded abroad. The parents of an English girl being treated in a Mexican hospital were threatened with her life-support machine being turned off as a result of their card being rejected for payments.*

---

* *A Case Study of the Royal Bank of Scotland IT Failures*, Global Association of Risk Professionals

The affected banks introduced extended opening hours at branches to allow customers, at least, to withdraw cash from their accounts. But what if there had been no cash to withdraw? What if all their liquid resources were tied up in electronic money, held in accounts to which they could not gain access?

Several times I have been affected by a meltdown of an electronic payment system. I have arrived in a supermarket or a restaurant to be told: sorry, we can't take cards, only cash at the moment.

The RBS technological meltdown of 2012 was no isolated incident. It happened to RBS customers again in January 2014, as well as to Lloyds' customers, when card payment systems went down for over three hours.* RBS suffered another failure in October 2016, while Barclays suffered a system breakdown in February 2017, as did the supermarket Asda in October 2016.

It isn't just accidental failures which can bring electronic payment systems to their knees. Over-reliance on them puts us at the mercy of deliberate cyber-attacks.

On 12 May 2017 over 42 NHS hospitals, along with hundreds of organisations around the world, fell victim to a piece of ransomware called WannaCry, which froze computers and demanded a $300 ransom for unfreezing them. Operations and appointments were cancelled. The attack was not sophisticated, and it happened despite Microsoft, which manufactured the systems that were being targeted, being aware of the virus. Two months earlier the company had issued a patch to protect computers from attack, but NHS hospitals turned out to be running old versions of the software which did not benefit from the automatic upgrades offered to newer versions.

* *The Guardian*, 27 January 2014

The attack was eventually foiled by a 22-year-old computer blogger who found a way of tackling it, but it left behind two lessons.

Firstly, that no one should assume that a large public body which has invested billions in computer systems and with an army of specialists to back up its technology is safe from cyber-attack. If it can happen to the NHS it can happen to banks, payment companies, retailers and anyone else.

Secondly, the attack undermined one of the favourite arguments of the cashless lobby: that abandoning notes and coins in favour of electronic money can help cut crime because the latter is traceable and the former is not. Brazenly, the hackers had demanded the $300 ransom to be paid in the crypto currency, Bitcoin. Bitcoin hasn't proved an entirely fool-proof currency for criminals – in 2015 Ross Ulbricht was jailed for life for trading $1 billion worth of illegal drugs in the currency after slipping up and revealing his identity.* Nevertheless, Bitcoin works with a high level of anonymity which forms the whole basis of its value in many users' eyes. The possibility of being caught certainly didn't bother the WannaCry hackers and they haven't been caught to date.

It isn't just criminal hackers.

In a cashless society we could be instantly prevented from accessing our money thanks to the mistaken efforts of law-enforcement agencies. Advocates of a cashless society argue that the ability to deprive criminals and terrorists of access to their money would be one of the advantages of a society without cash. But it won't so much be criminals and terrorists; it will be you and

---

* *Science*, 9 March 2016

I, falling victim to over-zealous, and not always wholly competent, actions on the part of the authorities.

That is what happened to Megan McArkle when she moved from Illinois to New York and the latter state lost her tax return. In error, its tax authorities concluded that she hadn't paid her tax and employed powers to freeze her bank account – requiring her to make numerous phone calls before she could have the mistake rectified and her accounts unfrozen. In a cashless society the error would have left her in a netherworld, unable even to buy food.*

In Britain, Ian and Jeanne Winspean suffered a similar crisis when their bank, the TSB, suddenly closed their accounts without any warning and without any explanation. The bank's anti money-laundering software had picked them out as suspicious.†

Why?

Because they kept moving sums backwards and forwards between accounts as they attempted to take advantage of a deal offering them 3 per cent interest – a rate reliant on them paying £500 a month into each account. For this rather crafty little enterprise the bank's algorithms had decided they might be handling money from a criminal enterprise and froze them out of access to their money. It was inconvenient enough as it was, but how much worse would it have been had there been no such thing as cash and they had been blocked from making any kind of financial transaction at all?

The cost to us in terms of time and bother when things go wrong doesn't tend to enter into the equation when the cashless lobby is trying to persuade us to use electronic forms of payment. We are

---

* Bloomberg, 18 March 2016
† *Daily Mail*, 27 June 2017

invited to concentrate our minds on the seconds we could save not having to fumble around in our pockets for change – without thinking of the hours it could cost us to put things right if our account is accidentally blocked, payments are made in error or anything else goes wrong.

There are the hours, too, which we must spend grappling with ever-changing technology. Although I wasn't born into the internet age I have come to use it heavily in my work. In many ways, I have come to depend on it. It has allowed me to work over long distances that I could not have done before. I use internet banking. I manage my investments online.

Do I wish for the days when I had to queue up at a post office in order to buy a road tax disc rather than spend five minutes buying one online?

Absolutely not.

The internet has hugely improved the quality of life in so many ways, part of which is the ease it has brought to financial transactions.

Yet would I want electronic methods of payment to be the only way I could buy things and settle bills?

No way.

While I am hugely appreciative of the freedom and opportunities which have derived from the world becoming connected technologically, I am also grimly aware of how technology can let us down. I know what it is like to be writing on a deadline and to find myself with a frozen computer, or with an internet connection that has gone down. I have developed ways of working which allow me to cope with full electronic failure – keep saving work to a USB, which can be pulled out and which, if necessary, say in the midst of a power cut, I can take to an internet café miles away and finish working there.

I know that I would not want my smartphone to become my 'electronic wallet', which would prevent me accessing my money every time the battery ran down. When I hear advocates of the cashless society argue that a phone can take the place of wallet I wonder if they have ever been outside an urban area, if they have ever been more than a few feet from a power socket where they can recharge their phone.

I wonder, too, if they have ever heard of arthritis, or can imagine any other physical condition which can make it hard for people to use smartphones with their touch keys.

While it may seem odd to intelligent young people who have been brought up to use computers and mobile phones just as previous generations used pen, paper and mobile phones, but nearly one in ten adults in Britain (9 per cent in the first quarter of 2017*) have never used the internet. Among disabled adults it is 22 per cent. For many with learning disabilities a smartphone menu is a way into a world they are always going to struggle to master – while they might more easily learn the shapes, sizes and values of coins. This is a group who would be seriously disadvantaged were physical money to be abolished. And yet their interests never seem to feature.

I am perfectly comfortable using the internet but I put myself in the category of people who struggle with a smartphone. To me, the ergonomics are appalling. I cannot pick the thing up without it performing some function I did not want it to perform. Often, the screen is far too sensitive – forcing me to spend time reversing

* *Internet Users in the UK*, Office of National Statistics, May 2017

what it has done. At other times, such as when I am trying to answer a phone call and am left desperately thumping the screen, it is not sensitive enough.

In common with about 5 per cent of the population I suffer from mild degree of Raynaud's Syndrome – where the blood supply reduces to the hand in reaction to low temperature. In cold weather my fingers produce virtually no heat – and so will not work a touch-sensitive screen. I used to have a Blackberry with tiny little keys which I could work, but to send an email on a phone with a touch-sensitive screen can take me half an hour. Others are faster, I am sure, but that is partly down to what they write. The predictive text function is helpful if you write like other heavy smartphone-users, a lot less so if you don't. Every time I write the letters 'B' followed by 'r' it comes up with the suggestion 'Britney Spears'.

❝ The smartphone industry seems to care little that a sizeable proportion of the population cannot use its product. ❞

The smartphone industry seems to care little that a sizeable proportion of the population cannot use its product. In 2015, only 18 per cent of the over-65s owned such a device. If you take, for example, the bed industry, it doesn't just manufacture beds for people who are young and athletic; walk into a bed shop and there are hard beds, soft beds, beds for people with chronic back problems, beds with weird contraptions which spring you upright – designed for people who struggle physically to get out of bed in the morning. Walk into a phone shop, on the other hand, and increasingly there is just one product: phones with touch-sensitive screens and no real buttons. Moreover, these phones are now sold with no instructions whatsoever. If you don't have the manual dexterity to use them, or a circle of friends to teach you their arcane language, there is nothing for you in a smartphone shop – you can just bugger off.

And yet this, the smartphone, is the device which the cashless lobby bases so much of its dream of a cashless society. It isn't just the ergonomics which make it hard to imagine how this would work.

I live in a rural area which can hardly be called remote: it is just ten miles from Cambridge, where so much of the UK technology industry is based. Yet even so the mobile internet reception is poor enough to make it a struggle to use a smartphone to connect to the internet. There are places I know – large areas of the Scottish Highlands, for example – which are far worse: there is no phone signal, let alone a strong enough one to bear an internet connection.

Even after 25 years of plastering the country with transmitters, the mobile phone industry has still failed properly to reach the homes of 17 million Britons, according to the British Infrastructure Group of MPs in October 2016.* In many of these areas it would be impossible to pay for things reliably via a mobile phone app. In some places not even a text message would get through. Coverage, according to the MPs, had not improved since 2014. Will it ever?

---

* *Mobile Coverage: a good call for Britain?*, British Infrastructure Group, October 2016

Some places will always be too hilly and too sparsely populated to justify investment in mobile phone coverage. Such places simply do not enter the calculations on many of those who advocate a cashless society. They are over the horizon, lost to the future that the cashless lobby wants to create.

If people want to use smartphones to make everyday purchases, they have the opportunity to do so. Yet in the developed world, with the exception of Sweden, we have largely chosen not to. The facility has been offered to us enough times. We have had Google Wallet, which has been around since 2011, Softcard (re-launched after initially being given the unfortunate name Isis), Apple Pay, Android Pay, Pingit. There are plenty of retailers who have agreed to offer the facility. Yet consumers have failed to get as excited by the idea as the advertising and publicity material suggests they ought to be. According to one industry survey only 17 per cent of UK mobile phone-users in 2015 used their phone to make a single in-store purchase – which was actually down on 2014 when 21 per cent said they had used their phone for this purpose.*

Why have so few taken up these services?

Security will certainly be an issue: do we really want to expose financial details in a mobile phone call which could be intercepted? But so, too, will be the sheer awkwardness of using a smartphone. Paying for things with cash or a card is easy. Why would we want to make life difficult for ourselves by first downloading an app and then having to fiddle around with the phone in the middle of a queue?

There will always be a few people who get a kick from using the latest technology and being seen to use it, but I guess most people

* *Mobile Payments State of Industry 2016*, Mobile Payments Today

take an entirely practical approach to assessing new technology: if it does make their life easier, or more fun, they will eagerly adopt something new. If it doesn't, they won't. I don't want to dampen the spirits of those who work in the financial technology sector, or 'fintech' as it likes to brand itself, but paying for stuff isn't the most exciting thing most of us do in the course of our week.

When I read and hear lobbyists pushing for a cashless society I wonder if it really comes down to one simple thing: so much money has been invested in fintech that there are an awful lot of financial interests who simply cannot afford for it to fail. Small wonder there are so many lobbyists pushing for governments to go cashless when, globally, venture capitalists invested $17.4 billion in fintech in 2016.* They are going to want a return on that money. And if we aren't voluntarily going to choose to use electronic forms of money, they are damned well going to try and force us to use it, by having cash banned. It is rather as if the fast-food industry, struggling to get people through its doors, had launched a campaign to ban kitchens in homes.

* *Forbes*, 17 February 2017

CHAPTER

*The
Negative Interest
Rate Trap*

THE STERN FACE of Lord Kitchener and his outstretched finger, imploring 'your country needs you', is one of the enduring images of the Great War. But after Lord Kitchener drowned at sea in 1916 – and with conscription earlier that year having made a young man's choice for him – another poster came to dominate the public realm in Britain. "If you cannot fight," it read, "you can help your country by investing all you can in 5 per cent Exchequer bonds. Unlike the solider, the investor runs no risk."

But he did.

The four million Britons who fell for the sales patter and bought 'War Loan' did their patriotic duty all right. In the early years, they seemed to have a good deal. Wartime inflation turned to deflation in the 1920s, and for several years the 5 per cent coupon paid on War Loan issued in 1917 must have seemed like the deal of the century. Holders were not to know that within a couple of decades these open-ended bonds, with no redemption date, were to be subjected to the financial equivalent of mustard gas.

In 1932, with Britain struggling to pay its wartime debt, the government set about a refinancing of War Loan. Holders were told that the bonds would be redeemed, but were offered instead a 1 per cent cash bonus if they converted to a new issue, this one paying a coupon of 3.5 per cent rather than 5 per cent. Given that the government couldn't afford to repay the £2 billion of War Loan it was a high-risk strategy – the solvency of the state was utterly reliant on most holders choosing to convert to the lower-paying bond. But it paid off. The vast majority dutifully converted their bonds, pocketed a 1 per cent cash bonus and looked forward to a secure retirement living off the income. Given that inflation in 1932 was running at minus 2 per cent, the new bonds were still paying a very decent return: a real interest rate of over 5 per cent.

It wasn't to last.

Within ten years, inflation had returned and the value of War Loan was on a long downwards trajectory which by the mid-1970s would lead to it trading at under £20 – less than a fifth of its face value. Thus, at a time when young, patriotic buyers of War Loan were living out their final years, their investments had dwindled. Ultimately, it was the holders of War Loan who paid for the first world war, via the erosion of their savings – not to the extent that holders of German and Italian war bonds had paid for their own countries' war efforts, by being wiped out completely, but by suffering a pretty severe capital loss nevertheless.

What diminished the savings of War Loan holders was a negative real interest rate. For decades, inflation ran ahead of the interest on the War Loan, producing a negative return. The government got to borrow its money cheaply – and the patriotic buyer of War Loan paid the consequences.

Governments would love to be able to set negative interest rates again. They would love to do so for two reasons: firstly, to help ease the pain of the huge debts that they have built up in recent years and, secondly, to help stimulate their economies, which have become sluggish ever since the financial crisis of 2008/09. In times of negative interest rates, governments can borrow with impunity –

it actually pays to be in debt. Moreover, interest rates are the main tool of monetary policy: raise them, making it more expensive to borrow money, and they might choke off an unsustainable boom. Lower them, making it cheaper to borrow, and you might stimulate a flagging economy. People will be more inclined to take out loans to buy cars, home improvements, holidays and what have you.

Trouble is, how do you reduce interest rates when they are already at near-zero?

The legacy of the 2008/09 crisis is an era of low inflation and near-zero interest rates. By the spring of 2009, in an effort to pull Britain out of the deepest recession since the 1930s, the Bank of England had reduced its base rate to 0.5 per cent – lower than it had been in 300 years. This was supposedly as a short-term emergency provision, but interest rates remained stuck there even as the economy began to grow again. In 2016, following the vote of the British people in a referendum to leave the European Union, the bank found an excuse to lower it further still: to 0.25 per cent. There it stayed, even though it soon became clear there was no emergency at all: the economy continued to grow strongly despite the vote.

In the US, too, the Federal Reserve set a rate of 0.5 per cent for seven years until a series of small increases in 2016 – and then only when rapid economic growth made the case for higher rates overwhelming. The European Central Bank went one further, reducing rates to zero in 2016. The overnight deposit rate went down to minus 0.4 per cent. By July 2016 the German government was issuing 10-year bonds with a negative interest rate of minus 0.05 per cent.* The following month negative rates had hit the retail

* Reuters, 13 July 2016

banking sector, with a community bank in Southern Germany, Raiffeisenbank Gmund am Tegernsee, becoming the first to charge depositors. Customers with savings in excess of 100,000 euros were charged a rate of 0.4 per cent – an annual charge of £4 for every £1,000 they saved.*

How indebted governments would love to go further and reduce interest rates still further into negative territory. The trouble is that they can't, really. Banks have run up against what economists call the "zero lower bound". If interest rates go much below zero depositors will start to ask: why are we handing our money to a bank when it is certain that we won't get all of it back? Why not withdraw our savings and keep it in the form of cash – i.e. banknotes – instead? There is some expense involved in doing this: the cost of hiring a bank deposit box or, if you are going to keep your money at home, a safe along with other security measures. But if you have 100,000 euros or more in savings and your bank is going to charge you an interest rate much below zero then these costs are likely to pale into insignificance.

How far into negative territory could banks lower rates before they found themselves opening their doors to Northern Rock-style queues of people wanting to remove their savings and keep them as cash? No one knows because the boundaries have not yet been pushed. But it is certain that there would be a tipping point.

Would you keep your money in a bank if it said it would deduct, each year, £50 of every £1,000 you had on deposit?

What if it said it would take £100? £200? Sooner or later you are not going to stand for it; you are going to join the queue and get that cash sewn into your mattress, or buried in the garden.

* CNN, 16 August 2016

But what if you couldn't?

What if there were no such things as banknotes to withdraw? What if money didn't exist in any form other than a bank deposit, and every single bank was charging negative interest rates? You wouldn't have an option to keep your savings intact. If you didn't spend or invest your savings sharpish, they would rapidly erode before your eyes. You would suffer the same fate as buyers of War Loan.

Some who campaign to abolish cash are quite open about wanting to pull off this stealthy raid on our savings. In his book, *The Curse of Cash*, Kenneth Rogoff is not the least bit shy of making the ability to set negative interest rates his main reason for wanting to phase out almost all physical currency. Following the economic crisis of 2008/09, he suggests, "optimal" monetary policy would have meant the US Federal Reserve lowering its main interest rates to minus 5 per cent, while the Bank of England and the European Central Bank would have lowered theirs to between minus 2 and minus 3 per cent.

But optimal for whom?

If negative interest rates had helped to stimulate the economy it would have been at the cost of raiding the savings of the financially-prudent. The reckless borrowers whose unaffordable debts had caused the meltdown of 2008/09, meanwhile, would have been bailed out – to an even greater extent than they were in fact bailed-out. The cost of this exercise would have been to provoke even more risky behaviour.

You don't have to try too hard to imagine the effect that negative interest rates would have had on reckless borrowers in the retail market. What, you mean you are actually going to *pay me* to borrow money to buy that BMW? Let's cancel that and I'll have the Ferrari instead. No, on second thoughts, let's have the Ferrari as well and the Beamer. And a Lamborghini as well, if you don't mind.

The rather dry arguments of Rogoff and others don't really address the emotional aspects of negative interest rates. To them, lowering interest rates to minus 5 per cent when inflation is zero is just like reducing them to 5 per cent when inflation is 10 per cent – both amount to a real interest rate of minus 5 per cent. But that isn't how it is going to be seen by the general public, or at least to that part of the general public whose eyes are larger than their financial tummies. To these borrowers, negative interest rates are going to seem like the economic equivalent of a perpetual motion machine, a device to allow you to go on treating yourself without ever suffering the consequences. And, as we found out to society's cost when the 2008 crisis erupted, there is no shortage of banks, when they are in the mood for lending, willing to feed reckless behaviour with cheap money.

I very much doubt, though, that banks in a Rogoffian cashless paradise really would be able to hold on to deposits. Just as reckless borrowers would seize on the opportunity presented by negative interest rates, so determined savers would be hugely motivated to conserve their wealth. Again, negative interest rates would have a significant emotional effect. It is one thing to tolerate a negative real return on your money; quite another to accept a negative actual return.

It doesn't matter how much economists try to convince people that minus 5 per cent interest when inflation is zero is no worse than 5 per cent interest when inflation is 10 per cent, people with a saving mentality are not going to see it that way. It is certain that they would find some way to conserve their wealth. If they couldn't hook out cash from their declining bank accounts and hoard it inside the sofa they would buy gold instead, or silver, or put it into bricks and mortar. That might boost parts of the economy – jewellery, developers, estate agents – but it isn't going to help oil the wheels of the economy in the sense that Rogoff imagines. All it will achieve is to inspire savers to investigate other stores of wealth, driving up the prices of these assets and distorting the economy still further.

The only realistic way out of the fiscal mess into which many developed nations have fallen is for governments to spend a little less and/or raise a little more tax so that they can balance their books. That might be politically unfashionable – damned as 'austerity' in Britain. But sooner or later they are going to have to find a way of selling fiscal discipline to their electorates. Trying to raid the savings of financially prudent individuals through negative interest rates, made possible through the abolition of cash, is no long-term answer at all.

CHAPTER

Snooping on Our Shopping Habits

E VERY SO OFTEN when I am trying to read the news on my computer I am faced with a pop-up box which, apropos of nothing, asks me if I am thinking of buying a car over the next few months. It took me a while to overcome my natural aversion to spinning lies and tell myself: look, I really don't have to answer this truthfully. If I do tell the truth, I have come to realise the consequence: if I let on I am thinking of buying a new car, for example, I will be bombarded with junk mail, spam email, cold calls, texts and everything else pushing at me some deal or other or imploring me to buy some particular vehicle.

And so I have learned how to fill in marketing surveys. Am I planning to buy a car in the next 12 months? No. How often do I eat out? Never. Do I go to the cinema? Nope. Would I consider travelling to Turkey on holiday? Not on your nelly. As far as consumer surveys are concerned I never buy anything and I am not interested in buying anything, ever; I have no hobbies, interests, friends or anything else. I am financially moribund, a non-consumer.

But what if, instead of having to ask me crude questions about my spending habits, the marketers had access to data on my actual spending habits?

What if, instead of knowing that I am vaguely thinking of buying a new car in the next 12 months, they knew that it is seven years since I last bought a car and that I have just paid a pretty hefty sum in servicing and repairing that now rather tired and creaking vehicle? Moreover, what if they could put that with the information that I bought a copy of a car magazine in W H Smith last week? It doesn't matter how much I lie to the consumer surveys; the real data on my spending habits will give the game away.

Imagine, too, if the marketers had access to data showing that I had paid by card to see the new Bond film last Tuesday, and Jason Bourne the Thursday before that? That lying bastard who says he never goes to the cinema actually goes every week, the marketing systems would say. Let's hit him with a string of emails and texts pushing the next Jack Reacher.

" Marketers have started to have access to the crack cocaine of marketing data: information on our actual spending. "

This is where the marketing industry is at the moment. It has been spying on our shopping habits for years, but until recently it has struggled for hard, direct data on what we have bought, and where. Instead, it has used lower quality data such as marketing surveys, subscriptions, memberships and the like. This it has used to classify us into socioeconomic types, based on our zip code or postcode. You might not be aware of it, but your neighbourhood might be classified on a marketing company's computer as an area of 'Top-Tier Auto Spenders' or, less-flatteringly, as an area of town inhabited by 'Struggling Families'.

But over the past few years marketers have started to have access to the crack cocaine of marketing data: information on our actual spending. They can get at this data because the card payments industry has realised the value of all the information it collects and has started aggregating it and selling it.

Mastercard, for example, has an information services division, Mastercard Advisers, which proudly claims to:

> offer access to relevant and actionable intelligence based on 95 billion anonymized, real transactions from 2 billion cardholders in 210 countries worldwide.*

This allows it to offer a product called Local Market Intelligence, which enables retailers to identify "average days between visits, repeat customer share and new customer behaviour".

Visa has a product called Visa Integrated Marketing Solutions which allows retailers to predict a consumer's behaviour on the basis of their previous spending patterns. According to the marketing bumf, it can help the retailer to ensure "that your offer is delivered to the right customer at the right time".† In other words, you innocently walk up to the shop checkout, contactless card at the ready to pay for packet of biscuits, and you find yourself offered a special deal on a bar of chocolate.

Why have you been picked out?

Because unknown to you, as soon as you tapped that Visa card on the checkout terminal the shop was instantly able to deduce what kind of consumer you are, based on your previous spending history.

---

* www.mastercardadvisors.com
† www.visa.com

American Express set up its Business Insights division in 2009 specifically to monetise the data gleaned from the spending habits of its 90 million customers worldwide. Every time you make a purchase on your American Express card it is used to build up a picture of what people living in your zip code or postcode are spending their money on. The information is then sold to third parties to help them with their marketing campaigns. As the smooth-talking marketing video puts it:

> You can find where your competitors are getting the most business so you can target customers in that area.*

While the data gleaned from our cards is already making big money for the payments industry, it is still limited in its extent. The trouble is that at the moment the cards industry is only able to collect data on about half of everything we purchase: the half which we buy on cards, or online.

When we pay with cash, on the other hand, we are anonymous; it could be anyone buying that bar of chocolate and newspaper. There is no way that the retailer can tell where we live, what else we have bought, how long it is since we last walked into the shop, whether we have been using any competitors' stores.

This is where contactless cards come in. They convert anonymous everyday purchases into a form from which data can be harvested.

In a cashless society we really wouldn't be able to hide. Details of everything we ever bought, where we bought it and when we bought it would be sitting on a computer somewhere, packaged up and sold to various commercial interests.

---

* *Getting to Know Insights Online*, American Express video

Does it matter that payments companies are snooping on our spending habits in this way and flogging the data?

Many people, perhaps, don't mind. If they are offered a special deal on a bar of chocolate they don't especially care how and why they were selected. Retailers, after all, are relatively benign institutions. Unlike George Orwell's Big Brother, they are not going to arrest us for thought crime. We are not going to get a KGB-style midnight knock at the door and find ourselves dragged off to a gulag just because we refused to buy a blancmange in their shops.

Yet how many of us really know what our credit and debit cards are really being used for, and how many of us feel we have consented to the use of data in this way?

The payments industry is well aware of the delicacy of what it is doing by using data on our spending habits. American Express Business Insights, for example, states on its website:

> Since this is actual spend data, it's important to note that we take customer privacy seriously. Our products consist of only aggregate information that is not specific to individual Cardmembers or Merchants.

What grates with me is that the payments industry tries to make out that a move to cashless payments is for our own benefit when plainly the industry itself has a huge amount to gain. Visa says of the rise in cashless transactions: "These trends provide economic empowerment to more people than ever before".*

Empowerment?

---

* *VisaNet: The technology behind Visa*, Visa website

It is not "empowerment" to have data collected on us, largely without our knowledge, and have it used to try to predict our behaviour in order to sell us stuff; a more apt word might be "manipulation".

❝ It is easy in Western democracies, where governments are relatively benign, to make light of privacy fears. ❞

It is easy in Western democracies, where governments are relatively benign, to make light of privacy fears. But the drive towards cashless payments is not just taking place in the West. On the contrary, it is being pushed far harder in many countries with more dubious records in handling personal data.

In China, the growth in mobile phone payments has been explosive in recent years, thanks to two smartphone-based services, Alipay and WeChat. Driven by smartphone-ownership, which has rocketed from 6 per cent of the population in 2010 to 71 per cent in 2016, mobile phone payments now account for 8 per cent of all transactions in China. Many people who have never had bank accounts are now routinely using their smartphones to make payments. The costs of using the service are low for consumers who link their phones to bank accounts but fall heavily on those without bank accounts – people using cash to top up their smartphone accounts with Alipay, for example, pay a 5 per cent charge for doing so. With merchants also paying a fee – usually 0.6

per cent of the cost of a transaction – smartphone payments have proved hugely profitable for WeChat and Alipay, which earned $2.5 billion and $7.4 billion worth of fees respectively in 2015.

The UN is hugely impressed, crediting the growth of smartphone payments in China with promoting "economic opportunity, financial inclusion, transparency, security and growth". But there is another sort of cost which Chinese smartphone users will soon be paying whenever they whip out their devices to pay for things: a cost to their privacy and, potentially, their freedom. The Chinese government has announced that it is to set up, from 2020, what it calls a "social credit system" which will use a variety of data to build up an individual's "social credit score" – which will combine what we would call "creditworthiness" with a more general measure of social conduct. Data obtained through smartphone payment systems will form part of the information used.*

The Chinese government is currently assessing several pilot schemes, one of which is run by Sesame Credit, a bank owned, like Alipay, by online shopping company Alibaba. The company is quite open about how the system uses data on financial transactions to build up an image of individuals which goes some way beyond simply assessing their creditworthiness. "Someone who plays video games ten hours a day would be considered an idle person and someone who frequently buys diapers would be considered as probably a parent, who on balance is more likely to have a sense of responsibility," the company's technology director has suggested.†

---

* *Social Networks, e-commerce Platforms and the Growth of Digital Payment Ecosystems in China: what it means for other countries*, Better Than Cash Alliance, April 2017
† BBC website, 26 October 2015

It is not hard to see where this is going.

For a government with an instinct for spying on its people the possibilities are enticing. You buy a bottle of rice wine and it will go down on your social credit score as a possible sign of alcoholism. Buy flowers and chocolates in a town far from where you live and it might be interpreted as a sign you are having an affair. Buy certain books in a bookshop and it might go down as a sign of possible dissent.

Is this really a healthy development?

As Chinese citizens are persuaded to give up cash in favour of electronic payments they are surrendering themselves to a novel form of surveillance: one which allows the government to use data on everything they buy to help build a personal profile of them. How might they wish in future that they still had access to cash and the anonymity it brings with it.

Seen through the lens of China's proposed social credit system, the remarkable enthusiasm for cashless payment methods among non-Western countries begins to take on a very different light. It begs the question: just why is the UN, which was founded in the first place with the aim of promoting human rights worldwide, so keen to promote the switch to cashless commerce – knowing, as it does, the means to which China is intending to put that data?

CHAPTER

12

Finding Guinea Pigs in the Developing World

T HE DEVELOPING WORLD is named so for a reason. On virtually every measure – wealth, education, sanitation, life expectancy – it lags behind the developed world. One day, hopefully, people in the poorest African countries will enjoy the living standards which people in Western Europe and North America do today, as technology filters down through the world's population. Sometimes the process can be given a kick start through initiatives such as producing generic versions of drugs which would be prohibitively expensive were they to be sold at the same price as paid by Western consumers and health services. But inevitably, as new technologies are developed, wealthy countries are usually going to enjoy access to them first, with others following as the cost comes down.

Yet there is one bizarre exception to this process. When it comes to paying for goods and services by mobile phone, it isn't American consumers who lead the way. It isn't European consumers, not even Swedes with their increasingly cashless society. The epicentre of the revolution in mobile phone payments is, perversely, the poorest part of the world's poorest continent.

Of the world's 300 million registered mobile money accounts in December 2014, just under half – 146 million – were in Sub-Saharan Africa.* Yes, a region where the World Bank estimates income per

* *State of the Industry: Mobile Financial Services for the Unbanked*, GSMA 2014

capita at just $1,630 compared with $41,230 in the UK and $57,540 in the US, is apparently outstripping all others in its progress towards a mobile phone-based cashless society. As for the region with the second-highest number of mobile money accounts, that isn't Europe or North America either – it is South Asia, with 76.9 million accounts.

How come?

The answer is that the cashless technology it is being pushed upon the population by an alliance of the United Nations, developing world governments, non-governmental organisations, charities and commercial interests. While Western consumers have shown some resistance to abandoning cash, the payments industry has found a rich source of consumer guinea pigs in poor countries.

The drive to turn the developing world cashless is being pursued with zeal by an organisation called the Better Than Cash Alliance, run by the UN Capital Development Fund. It is funded by, among others, the Bill and Melinda Gates Foundation, the Clinton Development Initiative, the European Bank for Reconstruction and Development, the International Rescue Committee, Save the Children and the governments of Afghanistan, Bangladesh, Benin, Colombia, Ethiopia, India, Kenya, Malawi, Pakistan and the Philippines. Oh, and Visa, Citi, Mastercard and Coca-Cola.

"We promote the transition from cash to digital payments in a way that improves lives and expands responsible digital services," declares the Alliance in its mission statement. Again and again it makes the assertion that a transition to cashless payments will empower the poor, especially women.

In April 2017, for example, Swedish fashion group H&M joined the Alliance, and said it would encourage its suppliers to pay the 1.6 million workers in its supply chain in mobile money or other digital forms. According to Gustav Loven, grandly-named Social Sustainability Manager at H&M group, the development would "increase financial inclusion and support women's economic independence".

There is a rather obvious incentive for Western corporations to involve themselves in a UN-backed campaign to switch the world's poor to cashless payments. In a 2016 report Visa is only too happy to lay out what it sees as the potential return on investing in the great drive to turn the developing world cashless:

> Given that fewer than 10 per cent of MSMs [micro and small merchants] in the developing world currently accept digital payments, they represent $35 billion in missed revenue every year for financial service providers.*

It goes on to say:

> In countries like Peru, sales by microenterprises alone represent as much as 20 per cent of national output. The vast majority of these transactions are in cash, meaning that financial service providers are not capturing the value that this sector has to offer.

It is clear, then, what the payments industry has to gain.

But what about the users of mobile money?

Among the initiatives of the Better Than Cash Alliance, in association with the World Bank Development Research Group, is a project to transfer workers in 21 clothes factories in Bangladesh from a system where they receive their wages in cash to one where they receive it in the form of mobile money in an account set

---

* *Small Merchants, Big Opportunity: the forgotten path to financial inclusion,* Visa 2016

up on a smartphone. In a press release from March 2017 entitled 'Why Women Workers and Managers Prefer Electronic Wage Payments in Bangladesh', the World Bank Research Group claims that smartphone payments have saved women the misery of the traditional payday when "often they must wait in lines, carry wads of cash through crowded streets or encounter a mother-in-law demanding money".

Let's leave aside the apparent sexism in a project which claims to be helping to empower women – why pick on mothers-in-law for their dastardly greed rather than husbands or fathers-in-law? The bumf goes on to claim that in one factory the 2500 workers had previously spent an average of 18 minutes a month queuing up to receive their wages in cash. This had cost the factory 750 hours a month in lost work time – all of which had now been eliminated.

Yet the press release also lets slip there was a snag.

While the factory managers had increased the productive time of their workers and no longer needed to transport truckloads of cash to the factory the overall cost of paying their employees digitally rather than in cash had actually gone up. The reason was that under the rules of the experiment the factories had been required to subsidise the fees which employees had to pay if they wanted to convert their digital money into cash.*

Every penny that had been saved in the factories – and more – seemed to disappear in the form of charges levied on the users of mobile money services.

There is a vast industry creaming off fees in this way.

---

* 'Why Women Workers and Managers Prefer Electronic Wage Payments in Bangladesh', World Bank Development Research Group, 8 March 2017

Across Bangladesh there are 550,000 agents making a living from helping people, many of them illiterate, to use the smartphone accounts which have been set up in their name. The market leader in mobile money in Bangladesh is bKash, a subsidiary of the BRAC bank, which has been handling smartphone payments since 2011. It now has over 50 per cent of the market. The bKash service allows users to make payments to approved merchants free of charge. But for other payments there are stiff charges. To withdraw money from the mobile account in the form of cash from an ATM machine costs 2 per cent. To withdraw cash via an agent costs 1.85 per cent. To transfer money to another registered user of the service costs a flat rate of 5 Bangladeshi taka (BDT).* The implication is that in order to transfer to someone the cost of a litre of milk (70 BDT) will incur of fee of 7 per cent.

To consumers in Britain, who are used to making basic transactions by debit card or BACS payment for free, these are eye-watering charges.

But these are just the official fees. They don't take into account the extra charges of which many users of mobile money in Bangladesh have complained. In 2015 USAID – the US government agency which oversees development projects – published a study into the use of mobile money, using a group of Bangladeshis who were working on US aid projects.† It depicted a group of poor individuals struggling to use a technology which had been pressed upon them and which they were ill-equipped to use. Unable to read the menu on their smartphone themselves they had been

---

* bKash website, 20 May 2017

† *Mobile Financial Services in Bangladesh: a survey of current services, regulations and usage in selected USAID projects*, USAID. April 2015

forced to use agents, whom they found sitting by roadside under large umbrellas. Too often, the agents simply ripped them off.

As one worker in Faridpur told the study:

> Agents frequently cheat village people. They withdraw money from the wallets of illiterate persons and inform them that their mobile money account is blocked.

The problem is that 40 per cent of Bangladeshi adults are illiterate even in their own language, Bangla.* But most of the phone menus which mobile money-users in Bangladesh are forced to use don't even use their own language – they are in English. Even when users could understand written English they often struggled. While smartphones are ubiquitous in Bangladesh – in 2015 there were 122 million mobile phone subscriptions, in a country of 156 million people – they are often trying to cope with a 2G signal. Many respondents to the USAID study reported that their phone would "time out" during a transaction, leaving them unsure of whether it had been successfully completed or not. Some found that their SIM cards had been deactivated through lack of use, leaving them unable to access their money. They were trying to use the phone to manage their finances, but found that financial transactions didn't count towards the minimum level of activity specified in their phone contracts.

Just why has a technology, with the UN's blessing, been forced on people who are least equipped to use it?

Far from promoting financial independence, for many people mobile money is doing exactly the opposite: it is making them dependent on agents simply to access their earnings. Four in ten

---

* *CIA World Factbook*

Bangladeshis have never had a bank account. What they could do with, in order to help them save and to protect them from theft, is basic, Post Office-style accounts with minimal charges. Instead, they are being made to leap-frog Western consumers and adopt a new technology with which even many literate and financially-astute people in the West are reluctant to adopt.

That isn't aiding development; it is using people in the developing world as guinea pigs for the cashless society which some would like, but have so far failed, to create in developed countries.

Bangladesh isn't, as it happens, the world's largest testing ground for mobile phone payments. That honour belongs to Kenya where, a decade ago, the country's largest mobile phone company, Safaricom, launched a cashless money transfer system called M-Pesa. It was born of an initiative between the British government's aid ministry, the Department for International Development (DfID) and Vodafone, the British telecoms giant which owned part of Safaricom. DfID officials had noticed that Kenyans had taken to swapping talk time on their phones as a proxy for money – a logical enough thing to do in a country where, at the time, only 12 per cent of people had a bank account and yet 80 per cent of people had a mobile phone. M-Pesa was an attempt to formalise what people were already doing, and proved hugely successful. By the end of 2016 there were 18 million M-Pesa users – in a country of 46 million – and an annual total of 6 billion transactions.*

There is little question that M-Pesa has filled a hole in the market in a country which has a poorly-developed banking system. One of its strengths is the ability to transfer money over large distances without the need for a bank account. Many Kenyans work in cities

* CNN, 24 February 2017

but regularly send money back to their families in rural villages and had previously relied on sending cash by bus in packages which all too often disappeared en route. A typical example of the beneficiaries is a Kenyan woman called Felista who works as a domestic cleaner in Nairobi but needs to transfer regular payments to her seriously ill mother in a distant village.[*]

M-Pesa is more secure than it at first sounds. A PIN is required in order to make transactions. Customers' account balances are ultimately backed by deposits in the country's large banks. While it is a lot easier to open a M-Pesa account than a bank account there is some form of identification required: usually an ID card or a passport.

Extravagant claims have been made for the economic benefits of M-Pesa. A study at the Massachusetts Institute of Technology, partly funded by the Bill and Melinda Gates Foundation, claims that M-Pesa has helped lift 2 per cent of Kenyan households out of extreme poverty – along with the familiar claim, which seems to permeate so much of the cashless lobby's case, that female-headed households have benefitted disproportionately.[†] Another claim is more straightforward to prove: competition from M-Pesa forced existing money transfer services such as Western Union and MoneyGram to reduce their prices.[‡]

Compared with Bangladesh, Kenya has higher levels of literacy – 90 per cent for males and 80 per cent for females. Moreover, M-Pesa is based on a simpler, text-based system which pre-dates

---

[*] *The Independent*, 20 February 2017
[†] *MIT News*, 8 December 2016
[‡] *Mobile Banking: the Impact of M-Pesa in Kenya*, National Bureau of Economic Research, 2011

smartphones. Nevertheless, M-Pesa hasn't been without problems. System outages were common in the early days, and still happen from time to time. Whether by their own error or system error, 4.3 per cent of users reported that money had been transferred to the wrong recipient, and a third of these had been unable to recover their money.*

As an additional method of handling money in a country with a poorly-developed traditional banking system, M-Pesa has been a welcome innovation. The problem comes when it starts to be touted as the basis for a cashless society. Were M-Pesa and other electronic forms of payment the only way to buy goods and services in Kenya it would be hard for anyone to claim that it was enriching the poor. The Achilles Heel of M-Pesa, as with many electronic forms of payment, is that it introduces charges into everyday transactions which were previously free. This is especially true at the lower end of the spectrum, on low-value transactions where the costs can swallow a huge percentage of the sum involved.

According to the published scale of charges which were current in May 2017 – excluding any unofficial charges which an agent might want to add on top – users who transfer between 101 and 500 Kenyan Shillings (KSHs) to another M-Pesa user are charged a fee of 11 KSH. That is equivalent to an 11 per cent fee if you are transferring the lower amount. Transfer between 101 and 500 KSH to someone who is not registered with M-Pesa and the fee jumps to 44 KSH – in other words if you are transferring 101 KSH (equivalent to US$ 1 and the cost of a litre of milk in Kenya) Safaricom will charge you 44 per cent of the value of that

* *M-Money Channel Distribution Case – Kenya*, International Finance Corporation

transaction. Withdraw cash from your mobile money account and you will be paying pretty stiff costs, too. Take out 200 KSH and you will be charged 33 KSH for the transaction – one sixth of your money will have been swallowed up.*

How could it possibly be in the interests of the poor if they were to be prevented from using cash and forced to use such a high-priced mobile money service for every single transaction?

No Western consumer would tolerate even nearly so high a charge. GSMA – a global trade body for the mobile communications industry – likes to quote a figure that the median cost of sending $100 by phone is $4, which it says is less than half what it costs to send money around the world by more traditional banking means.† But that is a figure and a comparison entirely irrelevant to most of the Sub-Saharan poor. They are not going to be making payments of $100 a time, and neither are they going to be making many international transfers. Rather more often they are going to be making tiny everyday transactions where the charges of paying by mobile money would consume much of their wealth.

There is another problem with the growth of mobile money in developing countries – where data protection laws are a lot looser than in the developed world.

As Bloomberg correspondent Chris Graeber found out when he travelled to Kenya to spend a few days trying to live entirely without cash, there is an inherent security problem in a transactional system which requires buyer and seller to exchange mobile phone numbers. After paying for a taxi ride, the rest of his trip was plagued by calls

---

* www.safaricom.co.ke, 15 May 2017
† *State of the Industry: Mobile Financial Services for the Unbanked*, GSMA, 2014

and texts from the driver wanting to know if there were any other journeys he would like to make.*

That M-Pesa keeps an electronic record of every transaction made via the system is often touted as one of its strengths. Potentially, it could lead to criminals being tracked-down, although if M-Pesa is helping to reduce fraud and money-laundering in Kenya there is scant sign of it yet – in 2016 accountants PWC placed the country joint-third in a survey of 115 countries for the incidence of financial crime.† In spite of elementary security measures, criminals have succeeded in defrauding customers through the sending of fake texts, which fool them into sending money to criminals.‡

❝ All mobile-phone-based payment systems have an inherent security flaw. ❞

All mobile-phone-based payment systems have an inherent security flaw. Phones emit signals which allow them to be tracked. In one system trialled in Britain, shops were fitted with tracking equipment which allowed the retailer to track the movement of each customer around the store – by latching onto signals from their mobile phones, without permission. It enabled the retailer to tell how long customers had spent in the store, at which displays they had paused to browse and which route they took around the

---

* Bloomberg, 9 June 2014
† *2016 Global Economic Crime Survey*, PWC
‡ GSMA press release, 21 February 2012

shop. Moreover, the information was stored so that the retailer would know how many times a customer had visited the shop on previous occasions.* This particular system didn't collect data on the identities of phone-owners, but clearly the potential is there to marry data from mobile phone purchases to data obtained from tracking your phone. Spend £1,000 in a shop and the whole town could be alerted that there was a wealthy consumer out shopping – along with your exact location at any one time. The Bloomberg correspondent's irritating taxi driver is just the petty end of what is potentially a vast seam of data extraction for commercial purposes.

Is M-Pesa really a rare case of a developing country leading the way in a technology which the rest of the world will soon be using?

" Taking away the right to use cash is not going to empower the world's poor. "

Not if South Africa is anything to go by. There, the service flopped and ended up being withdrawn in 2016 after not enough subscribers signed on. South Africans snubbed the service because they have much greater access to traditional bank accounts.† Banking services often are out of reach for the poor in the developing world. If mobile money can help fill a hole for people who need to make sizeable transfers of money over a distance, then that is a good thing. But it is a very different matter when international

---

* *Daily Mail*, 29 November 2011
† BBC, 11 May 2016

bodies and corporations start trying to use phone-based payment methods as the basis of a cashless society. Taking away the right to use cash is not going to empower the world's poor – on the contrary, it is going to take money from their pockets and make them dependent on companies who are providing the cashless means of payment.

As for governments which are trying to push their people to go cashless, we should not be helping or encouraging them. Going cashless is not a sign of material progress – if it were, the world's wealthiest countries would have done it long before now. It might, though, be a sign of a regime that is out to spy on and to control its people.

CHAPTER

13

Cashless and Unfree

W HY IS IT that so many of the countries which are keenest on creating cashless societies have some of the poorest records for respecting freedom and human rights? Scandinavia aside, the list of nations which are pushing hardest to eliminate physical money seems wearily familiar from the list of countries which regularly pop up in the news over human rights abuses. It stands somewhat ill at ease with the language of the cashless lobby, which tends to be all about "inclusivity", "empowerment" and – always prominent – women's rights.

Take exhibit one, Turkey, which has declared its intention of going wholly cashless by 2023. To this end, in 2016 the country's Interbank Card Centre (BKM) launched a new national payment system, Troy – an acronym of Turkish Payment Method – which is intended to become the basis of the economy of the new cashless Turkey. PayPal, which had previously offered Turks a way of making online payments, has had to pack up operations due to new rules which insist that servers handling financial transactions are based within Turkey. As a result, it has been refused a licence to continue to operate in the country.*

According to BKM, part of the purpose of turning the country cashless is to reduce the size of the shadow economy, which it puts at 26.5 per cent of national GDP. But if it sounds suspiciously like an attempt to control the population it is in keeping with much

* *Business Insider*, 1 June 2016

else going on in the country, where President Tayyip Erdogan narrowly won a referendum in April 2017 greatly enhancing the powers of the presidency and reducing the role of parliament as well as the checks and balances provided by the judicial system. A failed coup in 2016 was used as an excuse to dismiss 100,000 public servants who were claimed to have some kind of link with the plotters. A further 47,000 people were jailed on terrorism charges. Newspapers have been closed down and 150 journalists jailed.[*] The Council of Europe has become so concerned at what is going on in Turkey that it has begun monitoring human rights abuses in the country for the first time since 2004.

It isn't hard to see where a cashless economy fits into this picture.

It would provide Erdogan's government with a mountain of data to help keep track of its opponents. It would be impossible for Turks to pay for so much as a loaf of bread without leaving a data trail.

Or take exhibit two, the Philippines. In 2014 the Philippines Central Bank launched an electronic currency called the E-Peso, partly funded by US government's aid arm, USAID, with the aim of enabling citizens to trade and make financial transfers via their smartphones. There is little question that ordinary Filipinos could benefit from access to some kind of banking service. In 2013 it is estimated that 98 per cent of financial transactions in the country were with cash.[†] Yet the project seems to go some way beyond simply giving people the choice of using an electronic method of payment. The E-Peso website declares that its mission is "transforming communities into cashless societies". Lorenzo Tan,

---

[*]   Human Rights Watch
[†]   www.inquirer.net, 10 December 2014

the former President of the Bankers' Association of the Philippines declared upon the launch of the E-Peso in 2014: "The concept is to minimize the physical use of cash".

If the Philippines is trying to go cashless it raises the same problem as it does in other developing countries where mobile payment methods are being pressed upon consumers: it introduces fees for doing something – simply paying for things – which was previously free. As with so many other developing world mobile money services, E-Peso charges flat rate, per transaction fees which are disproportionately high on small-value transactions. For paying bills, E-Peso charges a flat rate of 10 pesos (16 pence or 20 US cents) per transaction – which is quite significant in a country where average household income in 2015 was 267,000 pesos* (£4,270 or $5,340) and where many people will buy goods in miniscule quantities, such as individual cigarettes.

But that might be the least of a Filipino's worries in the glorious cashless society that is being created for them. I would be more worried about the following statement on the E-Peso website:

> All transactions are recorded and can easily be monitored in a centralised database complete with user information, heightening transparency and tightening prevention of corruption and fraud.

I know that the Philippines has a problem with corruption and if I lived there I would want the government to do something to counter it – though not quite in the way President Rodrigo Duterte is going about it. During his successful election bid in 2016 he unashamedly stood on a platform promising to "kill all of you who make the lives of Filipinos miserable". He seems to have

* Philippines Statistics Authority

meant it, too. In the first five months following his election, the Philippines police's own figures record that 1790 suspected drug-pushers and killers were shot dead by police, while a further 3001 deaths were attributed to unknown vigilantes, which the police do not seem to be too interested in tracing.[*]

When you are going to take on armed gangs you have to be prepared for a bit of bloodshed, and I am sure that some of those killed were armed criminals who presented a threat to police. But perhaps not six-year-old Francis Manosca, who was shot dead along with his father by unknown gunmen who arrived at the door.[†] It seems inescapable, as Human Rights Watch and Amnesty International have both concluded, and in keeping with President Duterte's pre-election promise, that much of what is going on amounts to extra-judicial killing. In the same week that Francis Manosca was killed President Duterte himself boasted of shooting three men dead during his time as mayor of Davao.[‡]

Is this really the sort of government you want to trust with data on every one of your financial transactions?

And why is the US government funding a shift towards cashless technology when it is so clear how, in the wrong hands, such technology can be misused?

Exhibit three is Ecuador, the South American nation which adopted the US dollar as its currency in 2000. In 2014, it launched the world's first state-backed digital-only currency, ostensibly, according to a government official, to save itself the cost of having to replace dollar bills when they wear out – unlike a country with

[*]   Human Rights Watch
[†]   CNN, 16 December 2016
[‡]   BBC, 16 December 2016

its own currency it cannot simply print replacements; it has instead to buy them from US banks at a cost of $3 million a year.[*]

It is hard to believe that is the only reason for going cashless, though. Ecuador's introduction of a digital currency has coincided with growing authoritarianism.

In 2015, President Rafael Correa amended the constitution to allow himself to run for office indefinitely and to give himself greater control of the media, since when journalists have found themselves being threatened to "correct" their reports and newspapers obliged to carry government propaganda. Correa's regime, concludes Human Rights Watch, "continues to harass, intimidate and punish critics". When the people took to the streets in December 2015 to protest against growing authoritarianism 21 of them were sentenced to 15 days in prison for "issuing expressions of discredit and dishonour against policemen".[†] Again, this is not exactly the sort of government with which we might choose to share data on every transaction we make.

Exhibit four is Saudi Arabia where, according to Mastercard Advisers, the country's "cashless journey has been significantly spurred along by government leadership". The company goes on to praise regulations which have obliged employers to pay their employees via bank accounts and initiatives to turn the Hajj and Umra pilgrimages cashless.[‡] Developing a cashless economy is all part of "sustained and inclusive growth," Raghu Mahota, Mastercard's President for Middle East and Africa told a conference organised by the company in Dubai in 2017, and helping "financial

---

[*] CNBC, 9 February 2015
[†] Human Rights Watch, *World Report 2017*
[‡] *Cashless Journey Spotlight*, Mastercard Advisers, September 2013

inclusion percolate to the poorest, most vulnerable sections of society."[*]

All very grand words, though some might object that the word "inclusion" doesn't sit very well in Saudi Arabia, where women remain banned from driving cars (proposed to be lifted in 2018), are allowed very few opportunities to take part in sports and where they must obtain permission from a male guardian to marry or to travel.[†]

To its credit, Mastercard has invested in a Women's Entrepreneurship Program in Egypt and publishes an Index of Women Entrepreneurs which draws attention to the virtually invisible number of female business leaders in Saudi Arabia (just 1.5 per cent of businesses are owned by women). Nevertheless, a faster route towards inclusivity in Saudi Arabia would surely be for the country to liberalise its laws and to stop jailing and flogging critics of the government. Developing cashless payment systems, by contrast, at least creates the opportunity for governments further to suppress their people.

Then there is China with its previously-mentioned 'social credit score' – a proposed system for scoring every citizen on their trustworthiness and behaviour, with the aid of data captured from mobile phone payment system.

The governments who have joined the UN's Better Than Cash Alliance are not exactly models for human rights observance, either. In Peru, police are on trial for extra-judicial killings. In Moldova, £1 billion has been embezzled from the national banking system.[‡] In

[*]   *Saudi Gazette*, 1 May 2017
[†]   *World Report 2017*, Human Rights Watch
[‡]   Moldova Human Rights Report 2015, US State Department

Indonesia, Amnesty International has complained of "broad and vaguely-worded laws" which are being used to suppress freedom of speech and assembly.*

❝ Cashless payment systems are being used as a form of mass surveillance by governments, dressed up as a means of 'empowering' the poor. ❞

For authoritarian-minded governments, cashless payment systems are just too tempting a means to extend control over their population. Establish a state-backed electronic payment system and you can collect data on everything a citizen has bought, where he has been, with whom he has been associating. Cashless payment systems are being used as a form of mass surveillance by governments, dressed up as a means of 'empowering' the poor.

Worse, some of this activity is being funded by aid money from the West. Any organisation that is investing in, or showering aid money upon, cashless transaction systems ought to be asking: how could this technology be misused, and can we be absolutely sure that the government of the country in which we are investing won't be tempted to misuse it? In the rush to interpret cashless payment systems as a sign of economic and social progress, caution seems to be going to the wind.

* *Amnesty International Annual Report, 2016/17*

CHAPTER

14

What Would a Cashless Society Really Look Like?

N OT EVERY BANKER is mesmerised by the sight of dollar signs flashing before his eyes when the prospect of a cashless society is floated. Writing in 2013, Scott Shay, Chairman of New York's Signature Bank, described the abolition of cash as a threat to freedom. Without the option of doing business in cash, he argued, governments and corporations between them could quickly snuff out any business activity they didn't like. He cited the case of online betting in the US, all but killed off in 2010 when Visa and Mastercard, acting under pressure from the US government, decided to ban their cards being used to pay for online bets.*

He raised, too, the issue of 'civil forfeiture', the procedure in the US which allows government officials, merely on the basis of suspicion about an individual's financial affairs, to seize the contents of their bank account. In one case, a family-run grocer had its bank accounts frozen on suspicion that it was laundering money. Businesses are supposed to report if they handle large amounts of cash; the reason the grocery store didn't was that the cash going through its bank accounts fell just short of the threshold at which it would have needed to report to the authorities – it was, in other words, punished for being a small business.

If civil forfeiture is an illiberal measure now, how much more an abuse of power it would become if its victims did not have the

---

* *Cashless Society: a huge threat to our freedom*, Scott A. Shay, CNBC, 12 December 2013

option of doing any business in cash. They could be prevented from buying so much as a carton of milk on the basis of mere suspicion on the part of a government official.

It isn't just the likes of Turkey and the Philippines who can be relied upon to exploit the power that a cashless economy would give them; the US and every Western liberal democracy would do it, too. What, asks Shay, if a government decided to tackle the issue of obesity by programming card terminals in shops to reject the debit cards of overweight people if they attempted to buy food that was deemed to be bad for them?

Give up cash and we create huge opportunity for the manipulation of our spending habits.

Once you start to think along these lines, endless possibilities come to mind – things which have not yet happened but which you can be sure have occurred to someone, somewhere, in a government department or a company boardroom.

Give up cash and we create huge opportunity for the manipulation of our spending habits. Already, businesses are experimenting with the concept of 'surge pricing', where prices of goods and services are endlessly adjusted in response to demand – an example being taxi company Uber.

But what if those businesses had full access to data on the spending habits and financial resources of their customers? In a mobile phone-based payment system a shop could track your phone and send a salesman to meet you, adjusting prices, make special offers based on data gathered from your previous visits to the shop.

Buy a train ticket with a mobile phone and your movement around the rail network could be tracked at all times. If you got on the wrong train by mistake that could be picked up and recorded as a travel irregularity, enabling the train company to charge you a hugely inflated penalty fare.

Your home insurance company might obtain data on your spending and work out that you were out of the country when your home was burgled, allowing it, by some devious clause, to void your claim on the basis that you had spent more nights away from home than you had declared on the proposal form.

Tax inspectors might be able to obtain data on everything you have spent, allowing an algorithm to flag you as someone suspected of living above your means and worthy of investigation. It wouldn't be just tax cheats who fell into the trap but anyone who had saved up for something and spent more money than usual in a short space of time.

A state healthcare service could gain access to data on all the food and drink we had bought and use it to deny us treatment on the basis that we have failed to reform our eating or drinking habits.

Spending data could be used to enforce rules on housing – we could be forced to pay extra taxes on a property in which we had failed to spend the requisite number of nights to make us officially resident.

Not only could central banks set negative interest rates, they could also adjust those interest rates for individual consumers. Banks could advance us a mortgage on the condition that we didn't exceed a monthly spending limit – and then recall the loan if the data on our spending habits showed that we were exceeding those limits by eating out too much or going to the cinema. Or, if we missed a payment, they might exert their power to cancel our cards and our electronic accounts and prevent us from spending any money at all.

ʺ** To employ mass data collection in order to trap very minor offenders, or people who have merely made mistakes, is oppressive. **ʺ

Of course, arguments can be made why some of these powers should be used. The standard old defence of surveillance – if you have nothing to hide, you have nothing to fear – will be trotted out to justify snooping on the spending habits of tax cheats, petty criminals, and anyone else deemed to be antisocial. Yet to employ mass data collection in order to trap very minor offenders, or people who have merely made mistakes, is oppressive. It skews law-enforcement towards the smallest offences – which are easy to solve through surveillance – while doing little to catch the more serious offenders.

There is no point in anyone trying to argue that these powers will not be misused, because past experience tells us that if power can possibly be misused it certainly will be – just take the example of surveillance powers passed by Tony Blair's government on the understanding that they were to be used to trace terrorists, and which came to be used for the attempted prosecution of a Dorset couple suspected – wrongly as it turned out – of fibbing about where they lived in order to qualify one of their children for admission to a slightly better school.*

The question is, if we found ourselves in a cashless society where such oppressive powers were being used, would we tolerate it – or would we rebel?

What could happen is that we react by inventing physical currencies of our own.

Communities deprived of money always have tended to develop their own version. In a classic account of the economy inside a German prisoner of war camp in the second world war, published in 1945 shortly after the inmates had been freed and repatriated to their home countries, R. A. Radford recounted how at first the inmates would barter the contents of the ration packs they received from the Red Cross. Non-smokers would exchange cigarettes for chocolate bars, Sikhs would exchange tinned beef for other food and so on. Over time, a market developed with reasonably stable prices – a tin of jam being worth half a pound of margarine and so on. Steadily, all prices began to be quoted in cigarettes, which became a de facto currency. It acquired this status because it had so many attributes of the dollar bills which the inmates had used as money in the outside world but of which they were deprived in the camp: cigarettes came in standardised units, they were

* BBC, 2 August 2010

durable and instantly recognisable.* The money supply did waver – it diminished during times of heavy air raids when more people were driven to smoke the currency, with the same deflationary effect as a decline in money supply has in the outside world – but until the last few months of the war, when the ration packs failed to arrive and the informal POW economy collapsed, cigarette currency served the camps well.

Cigarettes also came to be widely used in US prisons – until 2004 when smoking there was banned. Thereafter, small packs of mackerel came to be adopted widely as a prison currency† and more recently noodles.‡

Commodity currencies pop up in schools, too. When I was a ten-year-old in the 1970s a craze developed for swapping things: toys, magazines, anything of interest to children. There, too, pure barter gradually gave way to a currency – in this case bottle labels brought in by one boy whose father brewed his own beer. Like cigarettes, mackerel packets and noodles, beer labels gained general acceptance because they were a standardised size and design.

What would happen if governments attempted to phase out physical currency and forced us to conduct our business entirely in electronic transfers controlled by large corporations who took a slice of our money every time we bought anything? It is a fair guess that the same would happen: ingenuity on the part of the public would find an alternative.

---

* 'The Economic Organisation of a POW Camp', R. A. Radford, *Economica*, November 1945
† www.wallandbroadcast.com
‡ CBS News, 23 August 2016

If any country other than the US were to abolish cash, and the US itself hadn't made this move, it isn't hard to guess what would become the de facto currency: the US dollar. It is already a widely accepted world currency, and has been adopted as the official currency of seven countries other than the United States, including Ecuador and El Salvador, and is widely circulated elsewhere, too. When I visited the Soviet Union in the dying days of that country in 1991 I didn't take roubles; I took US dollars. I never handled a single rouble on the whole trip; my dollars, on the other hand, were accepted with glee. I might be moved to take dollars next time I go to Sweden, too.

If, on the other hand, the entire world was to go cashless there is no shortage of other currencies which could emerge.

There is one commodity in particular which is widely respected as a store of value and which most people would have little trouble in trusting. It is, after all, already used as an investment of last resort in times of inflation or other economic crisis. It is gold. True, it is not always the easiest commodity to handle, but what if some enterprising soul were to start cutting, or melting it into small tokens, the value of which were stamped on the side? We could even carry them around in our pockets, and use them for everyday purchases. Yes, we would have reinvented coinage – but as a private currency rather than one sanctioned by the state.

It has happened in the past.

During the Californian gold rush of 1849 many of the prospectors who rushed westwards found themselves rich. Yet there was insufficient dollar currency in California to reflect the new-found wealth. The solution was for private mints to manufacture their own tokens, with a value in dollars stamped on the side. There are 450 different designs known to exist, bearing images of bears, Indians and other images, and either circular or hexagonal in shape.

The US government attempted to stamp out these private currencies with a Coinage Act in 1864 which outlawed the manufacture of tokens posing as official US legal tender. Private gold coinage was finally suppressed in 1883. But even then private mints got around it by removing any reference to dollars on the tokens, and carried on manufacturing them. They might have gained more widespread circulation were it not that by this time the gold rush, and the currency shortage it had created, was over. Americans trusted the dollar and so carried on using that. Although not legal tender, the coins which were manufactured have proved a pretty good investment. Decoupled from the fortunes of the dollar they have never been debased. Nominal $5 privately-made gold coins in the very best condition now sell to collectors for up to $100,000 each.*

Could governments prevent the development of private forms of cash in the event of their abolishing the official version?

Absolutely not.

They could ban tokens which pose as coins, but then what would there be to stop people trading in gold tokens which happened to be shaped like ear-rings? The government would have to ban ear-rings, too, along with all private-ownership of gold. But then we might start buying and selling things with silver tokens...

Currency exists thanks to trust. Without that trust, it collapses. If any government wants to try to push that trust to the limit, to tell us that in future we will have no option but to conduct our personal business electronically, via cards, tags and mobile

* www.pcgs.com

phones owned by private companies which are mining data on our spending habits, and to try to whittle away our wealth through negative interest rates, then its currency will lose that trust. Spontaneously, something else will emerge to take its place.

What would governments ultimately have achieved by abolishing cash?

To drive their people into using stores of wealth and mediums of exchange over which they had less control. Would they benefit financially from extra revenues as tax-dodgers threw in the towel, started using bank accounts and coughed up their full dues? I doubt it, but one thing is for certain: governments would lose a source of revenue which they enjoy from the issue of currency: seignorage. In order to distribute coins and banknotes, banks must in effect buy them from the central bank. The central bank can then invest the money elsewhere, earning interest on it. Every pound in our pocket is in effect an interest-free loan to the government. According to one estimate, the US government earned $70 billion from its issue of currency in 2015 – equivalent to 0.4 per cent of GDP.*

❝ *Every pound in our pocket is in effect an interest-free loan to the government.* **❞**

If I were the US government I think I would keep cash and be grateful, rather than chase the illusory benefits of a cashless society.

---

* *The Curse of Cash*, Kenneth S. Rogoff

Democratic governments who do try to go down the route of driving cash from the economy will find themselves in bad company, along with dictatorships seeking greater control of their populations. Ultimately, they may find the entire exercise counterproductive as alternative, private currencies emerge to take the place of legal tender.

CONCLUSION

T HE CAMPAIGN TO abolish physical money is often described as a 'war on cash'. At first that seemed to me to be a little over the top. Surely, I reasoned, what the payments industry was doing was just offering us a service which we could take or leave as we chose. The trend towards cashless societies was a form of commercial evolution which, for all its dangers, was ultimately driven by consumers, not by the corporations who dangle cashless products before our eyes. As for public authorities who were trying to make us go cashless, they were guilty of showing a little over-enthusiasm, but they weren't engaged in some sinister underhand plan to abolish cash by stealth.

But then I came across a paper written by the management consultants McKinsey in 2013, which itself used the term "war on cash".* That was how it described the first phase of a three-part programme which governments and public authorities should employ to drive cash to the margins. Incentives should be offered to those who want to pay electronically, barriers put up to dissuade people paying with cash.

Yes, it really is a war.

But it isn't a war where the B-52s are sent in to flatten everything in a display of shock and awe; it is a war where the infrastructure of cash payments is being gradually degraded through a campaign of precision strikes.

---

* *McKinsey on Payments*, McKinsey & Co, March 2013

To the public it might seem like a series of accidents – when you turn up at your usual car park to find it will only accept payments by mobile phone, when your bank sends you a contactless card and refuses to offer an alternative, when you travel to your local bank to find it is no longer allowing deposits of cash. But what is really going on is a programme of turning economies cashless by stealth. We wouldn't accept it if it were done in one go, so we have to be taken there by means of a thousand little *faits accomplis*.

But we shouldn't allow it to happen.

We should resist every move to turn our economies cashless. If we do not, we will cede control of our finances to corporations and governments. We will pay for this through high fees, through negative interest rates and in many other ways.

What is really going on is a programme of turning economies cashless by stealth.

We are continually told that going cashless is good for us, that it is for our convenience, that it will cut crime, that it will enrich us, that it will help to empower women and the poor. As I have argued throughout this book, these arguments are almost all spurious. Some cashless payment methods are convenient, others not; we are quite capable of deciding how we want to pay for things, without cashless methods being forced on us. The huge growth in financial crime is happening in the form of electronic money; abolishing cash will achieve nothing except to make vulnerable people more susceptible to online criminals. The poor pay far higher fees, proportionately, than do the well-off when they are forced to make cashless transactions.

How, then, to resist the cashless society?

We should insist on paying with cash when we feel like it. We should boycott businesses which try to ban cash and only accept electronic methods of payment. We should run up bills with them and, if they try to decline cash, go and dump bag-fulls of pennies in the foyers of their head offices. So long as cash remains legal tender, they will have to accept it. We should protest when public bodies try to turn services cashless. And, of course, we should protest to our elected law-makers, voting them out of office if they try to part us from our cash.

Of course, we don't always want to pay with cash. Often it is much more convenient to pay electronically. But when I see people meekly playing along with some new payment system which is tortuous to use and of no obvious benefit to anyone except the organisation we are paying, I wonder if they realise what they are really doing. I want to plead with them: don't fall for it. Don't let anyone tell you this is the modern way to pay and you are being a fuddy-duddy in resisting it. The electronic payments industry is doing its best to control us. We need to understand what is going on and do everything within our power to stop it.